COVENANT MARRIAGE

PARTNERSHIP & COMMITMENT

DIANA S. RICHMOND GARLAND & BETTY HASSLER

LifeWay Press
Nashville, Tennessee

© Copyright 1987 • LifeWay Press
Eighth reprint, 1999

ISBN 0-7673-9458-5

Dewey Decimal Classification Number: 306.8
Subject Heading: MARRIAGE

This book is the text for course CG-0199 in the subject area Home/Family
in the Christian Growth Study Plan.

Unless otherwise indicated, Scripture quotations are from
the *King James Version* of the Bible.

Scripture quotations marked NASB are from
the *New American Standard Bible,*
Copyright © The Lockman Foundation,
1960, 1962, 1968, 1971, 1973, 1975, 1977. Used by permission.

Scripture quotations marked RSV are from
the *Revised Standard Version of the Bible,*
Copyrighted 1946, 1952, © 1971, 1973.

The Scripture quotation marked NEB is from *The New English Bible.*
Copyright © The Delegates of the Oxford University Press, 1961, 1970.
Reprinted by permission.

Order additional copies of this book by writing to Customer Service Center, MSN 113;
127 Ninth Avenue, North; Nashville, TN 37234-0113; by calling toll free (800) 458-2772;
by faxing (615) 251-5933; by ordering online at www.lifeway.com; by emailing
customerservice@lifeway.com; or by visiting a LifeWay Christian Store.

For information about adult discipleship and family resources, training, and events,
visit our Web site at www.lifeway.com/discipleplus.

Printed in the United States of America

LifeWay Press
127 Ninth Avenue, North
Nashville, Tennessee 37234-0151

CONTENTS

The Writers 4
Introduction 5

UNIT 1

God's Plan for Marriage
    Lesson 1: Marriage as Covenant 16
    Lesson 2: Marriage as Promise 28

UNIT 2

A Journey Inward
    Lesson 3: Honoring Our Uniqueness 41
    Lesson 4: Celebrating Our Unity 53

UNIT 3

A Journey Outward
    Lesson 5: Called to Purpose 66
    Lesson 6: Called to Partnership 78

UNIT 4

A Partnership of Equals
    Lesson 7: Managing Anger and Conflict 90
    Lesson 8: Making Decisions and Resolving Conflict 103

UNIT 5

Commitment to a Partnership of Love
    Lesson 9: Love That Lasts a Lifetime 118
    Lesson 10: Focusing on the Future 131

UNIT 6

Couples Sharing and Supporting
    Lesson 11: Partners on Pilgrimage 144
    Lesson 12: Ministering Through Marriage 156

The Covenant-Marriage Movement 167
Christian Growth Study Plan 168

THE WRITERS

DIANA S. RICHMOND GARLAND

Diana S. Richmond Garland wrote the content material for *Covenant Marriage: Partnership and Commitment Couple Guide.* A native of Oklahoma, Diana is a professor of social work at Baylor University in Waco, Texas, and the editor of *Journal of Family Ministry.* Prior to joining the Baylor faculty, Diana served as the director of family-ministry research at Louisville Presbyterian Theological Seminary. Before that she served for 17 years at The Southern Baptist Theological Seminary in Louisville, Kentucky, as a professor of Christian family ministry and social work and as the dean of the Carver School of Church Social Work.

Diana holds degrees from the University of Louisville (B.A., M.S.S.W., and Ph.D.). She is the author, coauthor, or editor of 14 books and has published more than 40 professional articles.

Diana is married to Dr. David Garland, a professor of New Testament at Truett Seminary, Baylor University. They are the parents of two teenagers, Sarah and John.

BETTY HASSLER

Betty Hassler wrote the interactive learning exercises for *Covenant Marriage: Partnership and Commitment Couple Guide.* Betty is a design editor in the Editorial Section of the Adult Discipleship and Family Department at LifeWay Christian Resources, Nashville, Tennessee.

A native of Texas, Betty holds degrees from Baylor University (B.A.) and Southwestern Baptist Theological Seminary (M.R.E. and Ph.D.). She has written Bible-study units for adults and youth, interactive learning activities and teaching plans, and numerous articles for professional and family magazines. She was on the writing team that developed the original *MasterLife* materials, the first LIFE course.

Prior to coming to LifeWay Christian Resources, Betty was the discipleship and family-life director for Union Baptist Association in Houston, where she supervised support-group ministries and senior-adult, single-adult, marriage, and parenting seminars, retreats, and leadership training. She and her husband, Sim, have led numerous marriage-enrichment events. They have three children.

INTRODUCTION

Congratulations! You have just taken an important step. You have indicated that you are interested in learning more about your marriage and how you can enrich and strengthen your relationship with your partner.

This introduction explains the concept of covenant marriage, overviews this course, and stresses the importance of your commitment to complete the course. We will discuss the significance of marriage, trends in marriage, and the needs of marital partners. We will also examine the biblical concept of covenant as the foundation of marriage.

When you complete the introduction, you will be able to—
- identify current issues, problems, needs, and trends in marriage;
- write the implicit, unspoken covenant that is the basis of your current relationship with your spouse;
- describe the direction of this course;
- list expectations for you as a couple and for others who participate in the course;
- either make a commitment or decline making a commitment to be involved in this course at this time.

AN OVERVIEW OF COVENANT MARRIAGE
Covenant Marriage: Partnership and Commitment consists of this introduction and 12 lessons. The lessons are divided into six units of study.

A. Read the course outline below. Circle titles that sound interesting to you.

Unit 1: God's Plan for Marriage
  Lesson 1: Marriage as Covenant
  Lesson 2: Marriage as Promise
Unit 2: A Journey Inward
  Lesson 3: Honoring Our Uniqueness
  Lesson 4: Celebrating Our Unity
Unit 3: A Journey Outward
  Lesson 5: Called to Purpose
  Lesson 6: Called to Partnership
Unit 4: A Partnership of Equals
  Lesson 7: Managing Anger and Conflict
  Lesson 8: Making Decisions and Resolving Conflict
Unit 5: Commitment to a Partnership of Love
  Lesson 9: Love That Lasts a Lifetime
  Lesson 10: Focusing on the Future
Unit 6: Couples Sharing and Supporting
  Lesson 11: Partners on Pilgrimage
  Lesson 12: Ministering Through Marriage

You have indicated that you are interested in learning more about your marriage and how you can enrich and strengthen your relationship with your partner

THE PURPOSE OF *COVENANT MARRIAGE*

This course was designed to help you develop a stronger marital relationship with your partner. The Covenant Marriage program encourages Christians to exercise the promises and expectations of God's covenant love in marriage. This means offering each other steadfast loyalty, forgiveness, empathy, and commitment to resolving conflict so as to encourage each other in spiritual growth.

Covenant marriage is not a new concept. Throughout the Scriptures God's people made covenants with one another. Malachi 2:14 speaks directly about marriage as a covenant relationship. On the other hand, covenant marriage may be a new concept for you. If so, you are beginning an exciting journey. Along the way you will meet new ideas and have experiences that will challenge you to grow in your marriage relationship.

As you begin your journey, you need to take with you two pieces of baggage that will make your trip more meaningful.

1. Combining the word *covenant* and the word *marriage* makes this course distinctive. This course develops the idea of covenant as the foundation for marriage. When we think of covenant in the Bible, we immediately think of God's covenant relationship with His people—a divine-human covenant. Marriage is not a divine-human relationship; it is a human-human relationship. Even so, God's relationship with His people can provide us guidance in marriage. Part of the tension in this course will be discovering the characteristics in the divine-human relationship that apply to the human-human relationship of marriage. Along with the divine-human relationship, the Bible also contains accounts of human-human relationships founded on the covenant idea. Some of these relationships will be very helpful in our study.

2. Your second piece of baggage is almost just that—a container to collect and carry items in. There is a great deal to say about the implications of a covenant relationship in marriage. This course is based on the biblical and spiritual dimensions of relationship. You will be moving through the course selecting pieces as you go and placing them in the larger context of your marriage. You may not know what to do with each piece as you grasp it for the first time. Don't worry. The pieces will fall into place as you continue your journey through *Covenant Marriage*. This course offers an opportunity for you and your partner to nurture a strong, committed marriage relationship. Marriages built on the covenant concept give witness to the covenant love God offers persons through His Son, Jesus Christ.

To experience a covenant marriage, each spouse must have a personal covenant relationship with God. This is possible only by responding to God's revelation of Himself in Jesus Christ. When you hear the good news about Christ's death for your sins because of God's great love for you, you can respond negatively or positively. If you respond positively and receive God's gift of forgiveness and eternal life, then you become a child of God, and your relationship with Him is established. Without this initial response you wander through life without the knowledge of God and without His friendship and fellowship. Life is empty, for you have no sense of ultimate meaning and no sense of destiny. Though you are a creature of God, you are cut off from Him.

If you have not personally responded positively to Christ and invited Him to forgive your sins and enter your life, we encourage you to do that now. When you receive God's gift of Christ and accept His forgiveness, you begin a journey that will greatly enhance your marriage and the rest of life.

This course develops the idea of covenant as the foundation for marriage

B. If you have never committed your life to Christ, trusting Him as your personal Savior and Lord, read the information in the box below, "How to Be Born Again." Read the Scriptures and repeat the prayer for salvation. Follow up your commitment by becoming an active part of God's church. Talk to a minister about your decision.

HOW TO BE BORN AGAIN

1. "All have sinned, and come short of the glory of God" (Romans 3:23). Everyone is a sinner; there are no exceptions.
2. "The wages of sin is death; but the gift of God is eternal life through Jesus Christ our Lord" (Romans 6:23). Death means separation forever from God. Eternal life comes by trusting Jesus Christ.
3. "But God commendeth his love toward us, in that, while we were yet sinners, Christ died for us" (Romans 5:8). God loved us sinners so much that He gave His Son to die for our sins.
4. "If thou shalt confess with thy mouth the Lord Jesus, and shalt believe in thine heart that God hath raised him from the dead, thou shalt be saved" (Romans 10:9). To be born again, you must believe that Jesus died for your sins and must declare that you accept Him as Lord of your life.
5. "For whosoever shall call upon the name of the Lord shall be saved" (Romans 10:13). God promises you that if you accept Jesus as Lord, He will accept you. Call on the Lord now as you pray this prayer:
   Dear God, I know that I have sinned by breaking Your laws, and I ask for Your forgiveness. I believe that Jesus died for my sins. I want to be born again and receive new life in Him. I will follow Jesus as my Lord and will seek to obey Him in all I do. In Jesus' name I pray. Amen.

C. As you read the following purposes of *Covenant Marriage,* draw stars beside those you would like to develop in your marriage.

This course will help you—
- gain a better understanding of love and forgiveness in marriage;
- know how you and your spouse are alike and different and learn how these similarities and differences can become a source of relational growth;
- handle feelings of anger and manage conflict in ways that strengthen rather than destroy marital intimacy;
- use contracts for change that strengthen your covenant with each other;
- handle crises and stress so that your marriage grows stronger even in times of trouble;
- encourage each other to share your thoughts and feelings;
- support and encourage each other's individuality;
- recognize in what ways God has called you as a couple into a ministry partnership;
- strengthen relationships among couples and families in your church who can offer support and encouragement to one another in living covenant responsibilities;
- put into action the basic principles and guidelines you learn.

God promises you that if you accept Jesus as Lord, He will accept you

Covenant Marriage: Partnership and Commmitment is a part of the LIFE (Lay Institute for Equipping) learning system. LIFE courses enable Christians to grow at their own pace and develop skills and competencies in various areas according to their life callings and spiritual gifts. Each LIFE course includes individual study and real-life experience. A weekly small-group session brings the two together as participants discuss and reflect on their learning and practice new skills with one another.

YOUR COUPLE GUIDE
This *Couple Guide* will be a valuable tool for you as you work through this course. You may have received it before attending the introductory session. If so, you should complete this introduction before attending and pray about your involvement in the course. If you did not receive the guide early, that's fine. Your leader will share expectations for you and him or her during the introductory group session.

You will work through your *Couple Guide* on your own at home, one lesson at a time, by reading each lesson and completing the learning activities. Both you and your spouse should each have a copy so that you can make personal notes and complete the written activities. At times you will compare, reflect on, and discuss your responses to the activities with your spouse.

Do not simply read the *Couple Guide* without completing the activities and assignments. To do so would short-circuit the learning process and keep you from achieving the goals of the course. The activities and assignments are just as important for your learning as reading the written material.

As you complete the activities in this guide, write exactly what you feel. Sometimes the act of writing helps clarify our thinking.

This guide is your private property. Like a journal, it should be read only by those you grant permission. Make an agreement with your mate and other family members that your *Couple Guide* is not for their general reading. You will never be asked to share the information you have written in a group session unless you voluntarily do so.

The course includes a one-hour group session to follow each lesson. Complete the lesson or lessons that will be covered before attending the group session.

In addition to your individual work in this guide, you will spend time putting into practice what you have learned with your partner. You and your partner will work on many activities together and will also discuss what you have read and experienced in the group sessions. The results will be well worth your investment of time and energy.

You will spend time putting into practice what you have learned with your partner

D. Summarize what will be expected of you if you continue this course.

_____

_____

THE SIGNIFICANCE OF MARRIAGE
Whether you have been married for 20 weeks or 20 years, you know how important marriage is in your life. Marriage is the one relationship in our lifetime that is expected to last "until death do us part." Most of us outlive our parents; our children are in our homes for only a short 20 years or so before they center

their lives elsewhere; friends may come and go. We expect our marital partners, on the other hand, to be the hub of family for us when others have moved on. Because people are living longer, many marriages last more than half a century.

Marriages are not only long relationships but also broad relationships. We share many aspects of our lives with our partners. Our shared life shapes our habits, values, and ways of thinking. We share everything from a bed to a bank account, and we work with each other on everything from decorating our home to disciplining children. Through the years our experiences together, as we live our lives in tandem, shape and mold even our personalities.

Finally, we expect marriage to be a deeply intimate relationship. We stand naked before each other unashamed (see Genesis 2:25); no one else knows us as well as our marital partner. Marriage is created by God to provide companionship in a lonely world (see Genesis 2:18).

Length, breadth, and depth—all three describe the significance of marriage. Perhaps no other decision we make in a lifetime has the impact that committing ourselves to a marriage relationship does. There are bound to be times of frustration, of feeling overwhelmed by the promises we have made and the task that faces us as a couple. *Covenant Marriage* was not designed to add to the burden of responsibility and expectations that come with marriage. Instead, *Covenant Marriage* recognizes that our imperfect attempts to love each other can be transformed by God's grace into a relationship that bears the stamp of our covenant with the Father through the love of Christ.

E. How long have you been married? _____ How old will you be when you have been married for 50 years? _____

Do you and your mate share every aspect of your lives with each other?
❑ Yes ❑ No

Would you describe your marriage as an intimate relationship? ❑ Yes ❑ No

TRENDS IN MARRIAGE

Current trends in marriage have brought regular media attention to the question, What is happening to the family? If they know no other statistic, most people know current divorce statistics. Some of the trends in marriage that give us cause for worry include—
- ever-rising divorce statistics;
- more people than ever deciding not to marry at all;
- some states considering legitimizing "term marriages," marriages that are time-limited, not lifetime commitments, that may or may not be renegotiated when the contract expires;
- half of all children spending some time in single-parent homes;
- high rates of premarital sexual experience, pregnant brides, and marital infidelity;
- increasing awareness of high levels of family violence, with a significant percentage of marriages reporting some kind of violence during any given year.

Underneath this restlessness in American marriage is the increasing expectation that the marital relationship will bring deep satisfaction and great happiness through a lifetime together. Yet in almost every marriage come times of dissatisfaction and unhappiness. Making a covenant with each other does not

Perhaps no other decision we make in a lifetime has the impact that committing ourselves to a marriage relationship does

ensure living happily ever after. The challenges of different needs and values and of conflicting life patterns face even the most loving and committed couple.

THE NEEDS OF COUPLES

Most spouses have had little direct education in the art and skills of nurturing a marriage. Perhaps the most significant training we have for marriage comes from observing our parents' marriage. Our expectations of marriage, as well as our ways of handling intimacy and conflict, often reflect the relationship patterns of our parents. Particularly during times of stress when it is hard to think clearly about what we want to say or do, we fall into the behavior patterns we observed so many years in Mom and Dad. If our parents were loving, committed persons who modeled effective conflict skills, the patterns may serve us well. Even so, every marriage is different; every marriage has its own needs and patterns of living, which grow strongest with conscious effort from both partners.

F. How have the role models of your and your partner's parents affected your marriage? Circle one.

significant effect   some effect   insignificant effect

Every marriage has strong points, and every marriage has areas in which growth and change are needed. *Covenant Marriage* will help you celebrate your strengths and understand and work toward meeting your needs as covenant partners.

G. Name at least one strength of your marriage relationship.

_____

Name one area of your marriage in which you would like to see growth and change.

_____

SHARING NEEDS WITH OTHER COUPLES

How can talking with other couples about marriage be helpful? As many friends as you may have, you probably rarely talk with them about your marriage except in general terms. It is taboo in our culture to tell other people about the inner workings of our marriage relationship. We may make jokes about our marriage, and we may even gossip about our spouse to our close friends or parents. But we almost never share our marital concerns and joys in a serious way with friends and family to seek God's purposes in our marital relationship. We are more likely to share in this way about our children, work, church, and friends than we are about our marriage.

H. Check the statement that reflects your opinion.
❏ I think my marriage is happier than most.
❏ I think my marriage is as happy as most.
❏ I think others are more happily married than I am.

Every marriage has strong points, and every marriage has areas in which growth and change are needed

10

We risk a great deal when we share with others the needs and joys of our marriage. Because marriage involves so much of our lives, sharing about marriage really means sharing a great deal of ourselves. Yet there is so much to be gained from sharing. The Bible encourages us to bear one another's burdens.

When we share with one another, we find out that we are not alone in our troubles:
- "I can't believe that all those other couples argue the way we do about chores such as who does the dishes and who picks up!"
- "I'm glad other people enjoy being with their parents, too. I've always felt strange that we enjoy spending so much time with our folks, that maybe we were too tied to our families. I feel good now."
- "It's really all right for us to enjoy being apart in addition to spending time together."

Sharing with others also exposes us to new options and possibilities:
- "How do you and your husband take care of the endless errands—dry-cleaning, kids' doctor appointments, getting appliances fixed—with both of you working?"
- "Instead of trying to be together in the evenings with the kids and their friends in and out and the phone ringing, I'd like us to get up earlier and just the two of us have breakfast together, as Susan and Mike do."

Throughout *Covenant Marriage* the guidelines and activities will help you apply the ideas you discover through reading and sharing with others in the group. The Holy Spirit can influence your daily relationship with each other as you study the Bible, pray, and share your experiences with other couples.

I. **How do you feel about the prospect of sharing your thoughts and feelings with a marriage-enrichment group? Check the words that apply.**

| ❏ excited | ❏ anxious | ❏ hesitant | ❏ willing | ❏ worried |
| ❏ scared | ❏ eager | ❏ pleased | ❏ wondering | |

COVENANT: THE FOUNDATION OF CHRISTIAN MARRIAGE
This course stands on the biblical concept of covenant. An understanding of covenant from the biblical perspective will reveal ways marriage is a covenant relationship.

What Is a Covenant?
A covenant is a relationship bound by steadfast love, faithfulness, and devotion. The heart of a covenant is not rights and responsibilities but steadfast love that never ceases (see Lamentations 3:22-23). Rights and responsibilities grow from covenant relationships characterized by steadfast love, faithfulness, and devotion. A covenant means that two persons will act in love toward each other unconditionally. It is not giving and receiving love as long as you measure up as a partner and do all the things a good spouse should do. It is love freely given, whether or not it is earned or deserved, just as God loves us whether or not we deserve it.

God has related to people through divine-human covenants from the formation of the people of Israel to the new covenant sealed with the death and resurrection of Jesus Christ. Human-human covenants of steadfast love and loyalty provide the most moving accounts of personal relationships in the Bible, as seen in the lives of Ruth and Naomi, David and Jonathan, and Rahab

A covenant is a relationship bound by steadfast love, faithfulness, and devotion

and the Israelite spies. Both types of biblical covenants (divine-human and human-human) demonstrate that covenants are not just public promises we make but commitments to act lovingly and loyally no matter what the cost.

Covenant relationships are based on the decision to act in love, not on feelings. They are not the outgrowth of "falling in love," with the rapid heartbeat and deep sighs we associate with lovesickness. Instead, a covenant is faithfulness in action. Did Ruth feel like leaving her homeland and family? As Jesus prayed in the garden of Gethsemane, was He excited and thrilled at the prospect of being crucified as He thought about what lay ahead? Living in covenant means acting responsibly and lovingly even when our feelings want to take us in a different direction.

Covenant love and care for each other in marriage mirror God's love and care for us. As we look at God's covenant promises, we catch a glimpse of the image that marriage is to have. God's covenant endures—nothing can separate us from the love of God (see Romans 8:38-39). God's covenant is love freely offered to us through Jesus Christ. Covenant marriage is an opportunity to witness to our Lord's grace and love as we demonstrate the transforming power of God's love in human relationships. As we live in covenant with each other, we are also living in covenant with God, for "by this all men will know that you are my disciples, if you have love for one another" (John 13:34-35, NASB).

The promises of covenant marriage include unconditional love, forgiveness, comfort, and hope. We cannot fulfill these promises to each other alone. God promises blessings of mercy and grace more than sufficient to overcome our weaknesses and sinfulness as marital partners. Covenant marriage is not possible without God.

God promises blessings of mercy and grace more than sufficient to overcome our weaknesses and sinfulness as marital partners

J. Check the following words that describe the heart of covenant marriage.
- ❑ steadfast
- ❑ mutual
- ❑ mirrors God's love
- ❑ forgiving
- ❑ conditional
- ❑ rights and responsibilities
- ❑ based on feelings
- ❑ freely given

Covenant-Marriage Principles

From the biblical images of covenant come several principles that guide us in living in covenant marriage.
1. Marriage is a gift of God, and this is cause for celebration.
2. We are called to fulfill our gifts and responsibilities both in and outside marriage.
3. Marriage pictures the way God loves and covenants with persons and should reflect God's love, forgiveness, and grace.
4. Covenant partners' love is based not on feelings but on loving decisions and actions.
5. Covenants are unconditional commitments, not contracts based on mutual obligations.
6. Covenant partners share responsibility for meeting each other's needs and for answering God's call to minister to others through their relationship.
7. Partners grow spiritually as they live their covenant promises with each other.
8. Marriage balances difference and similarity, separateness and unity.
9. The relationship between covenant partners is directed by love, not power, and by responsibilities, not rights.

10. Every covenant marriage has a unique identity and a unique meaning and purpose in the mind of God.
11. Conflict is a natural part of a marital relationship and can be a source of relational growth and increased intimacy.
12. Covenant partners need the support and the opportunities to minister that come with being a part of a larger community of faith.

K. Look back over the list of principles of covenant marriage. List the three you would most like to characterize your marriage.

1. _____

2. _____

3. _____

Here is an example of the type of covenant that grows from the covenant-marriage principles presented in this course.

> Believing that marriage is a covenant intended by God to be a lifelong relationship between a man and a woman, we vow to God, each other, our families, and our community to remain steadfast in unconditional love, reconciliation, and sexual purity, while purposefully growing in our covenant-marriage relationship.

One goal of this course is that you and your spouse develop and commit yourselves to a covenant that expresses your unique commitment to each other. You will begin this process in the introductory group session.

YOUR COMMITMENT TO *COVENANT MARRIAGE*
The effectiveness of this *Covenant Marriage* course depends on your personal commitment to prepare for, attend, and participate in every session. Participants in the course will learn not only from the written material and the leader but also from one another. If you decide to be a part of the group, your attendance and preparation will be important not only to you and your partner but to the other participants as well.

L. If you are willing to devote your best efforts to completing the course, complete the following commitment by signing your name and dating it.

> Recognizing the value of *Covenant Marriage*, I commit to prepare for, attend, and participate in each group session. If I am unable to attend a session, I will seek my leader's assistance in completing the session's materials.
>
> _____   _____
>   Signature   Date

Marriage is a covenant intended by God to be a lifelong relationship between a man and a woman

Perhaps you are aware that personal, family, or professional responsibilities in your life at this time will make it difficult for you to commit time for preparation and regular group sessions. You may decide that this is not the time to commit yourself to a course like *Covenant Marriage*. Prayerfully reconsider the study of *Covenant Marriage* at another time.

M. If you are not prepared to commit yourself to *Covenant Marriage* at this time, what seems to be the primary reason?

_____

What needs to happen before you can commit yourself to this course?

_____

_____

SUMMARY

Covenant Marriage is like other marriage-enrichment courses because it enables each couple to achieve maximal happiness and satisfaction from their marriage relationship. *Covenant Marriage* is unlike other marriage-enrichment courses because it is based on the biblical and spiritual dimensions of relationship that make real joy possible.

In this lesson you have been introduced to the idea of covenant as the foundation for marriage. This may be a new concept for you. Perhaps it simply affirms what you already believe about marriage. In either case we all need information, understanding, and practice in skills that can help us make a covenant relationship a reality for our marriage.

LOOKING AHEAD

There is much more to say about the implications of a covenant relationship in marriage! In lesson 1 we will describe the characteristics of a covenant relationship, based on the biblical concept of covenant.

Covenant Marriage is based on the biblical and spiritual dimensions of relationship that make real joy possible

UNIT 1

GOD'S PLAN FOR MARRIAGE

MARRIAGE AS COVENANT

Lesson 1

Despite whatever problems or short-comings there may be, family and church relationships are good gifts from God

The introduction described the direction of this course of study and explained the expectations for you and the group. You were asked to commit yourself to this exciting and challenging growth opportunity. We commend you on your decision to continue.

Recall some of the current issues and trends in marriage today that were presented. What assumptions that you brought into your marriage did you uncover? Review the covenant you formulated that represents the basis of your current relationship with your spouse.

OVERVIEW

Lesson 1 introduces the concept of marriage as a covenant relationship. You will discover how a covenant differs from a contract by examining the covenants between persons in the Bible. You will identify characteristics of a covenant relationship.

When you complete this lesson, you will be able to—
* define *covenant* and contrast it with contract;
* list six characteristics of a covenant relationship, based on the biblical concept of covenant;
* describe the way the concept of covenant applies to marriage;
* rewrite your covenant with your spouse, based on your new understanding of covenant.

COVENANTS BETWEEN PERSONS

A child began evening prayers with "Thank You, God, for Mommy and Daddy." A deacon began a Sunday-morning prayer with "I thank You for the opportunity to gather in this fellowship of believers to worship You." The child and the deacon recognized that, despite whatever problems or shortcomings there may be, family and church relationships are good gifts from God. Do we say similar prayers of thanksgiving for our marriages? At times we lose sight of marriage as "a good thing" (Proverbs 18:22). We may be too focused on the tasks that need to be done, the problems we need to resolve, or the ways our partners ought to change.

The story of creation teaches that the relationship between man and woman is part of God's good work, a gift to keep us from being lonely (see Genesis 2:18).

Someone once said that a good marriage is "just talking." Of course, there is more to marriage than talking and listening, but it is a blessing to have someone to talk with who is really interested in the joys and disappointments of daily life. Marriage is a blessing from God and calls for thanksgiving (see Genesis 2:23a).

In what ways has your marriage been a gift from God? Despite disappointments and hurts, there have been times of sharing—joy in shared parenting, shared work (hanging wallpaper or growing a garden, ministry together through church or in community), shared family relationships (relatives-in-law who have added to your sense of belonging and given you others to care for in return), and shared intimacy.

A. List three ways your marriage has been a good gift from God.

1. _____

2. _____

3. _____

Pause now and thank God specifically for these three good gifts.

In the Bible marriage is not only a good gift, but it also illustrates God's covenant with people. We relate to God not as to some distant power in the universe but with the love and loyalty and acts of devotion expected in the intimate relationship of marriage (see Jeremiah 2:2; 3:1,6-8; Ezekiel 16:8-32; Hosea 2: 7-8,19-20; Mark 2:18-20; Ephesians 5:21-33; 2 Corinthians 11:2). God covenanted with Israel; marriage is a covenant between a man and a woman (see Malachi 2:14; Ezekiel 16:8; Proverbs 2:16-17).

B. Read the Scriptures on the left and match each with a description on the right.
___ 1. Malachi 2:14   a. God's covenant with Israel is compared to a marriage covenant.
___ 2. Ezekiel 16:8   b. God is a witness to your marriage covenant.
___ 3. Proverbs 2:16-17 c. A wayward partner ignores the marriage covenant made before God.

In receiving God's good gift of marriage, we also accept the responsibility of living in a covenant relationship that illustrates our covenant with God

In receiving God's good gift of marriage, then, we also accept the responsibility of living in a covenant relationship that illustrates our covenant with God.

Usually, we think of a covenant strictly as a contract, an agreement, or a promise that is solely based on rights and responsibilities. In our culture, marriage is a legal contract that requires a legal license to begin and a legal process to dissolve. The biblical concept of covenant, however, is quite different.

In the Bible a covenant between persons or between the nation Israel and Yahweh was the formal expression of a relationship bound by steadfast love, faithfulness, and devotion. The heart of a covenant was not rights and responsibilities but "the steadfast love of the Lord," which "never ceases" (Lamentations 3:22, RSV). Rights and responsibilities grew from the covenant and pertained to the confirmation and administration of the covenant relationship.

The Bible includes many accounts of covenants. In this lesson we will examine the human-human covenants between persons in the Bible. In lesson 2 we will look at our divine-human covenant with God. Looking at biblical covenants between persons, we find the following guidelines useful for directing our relationship in covenant marriage.

Covenants are the fruit of a loving, faithful relationship. Your relationship with each other did not begin when you said wedding vows. The vows came as the fruit of a growing commitment and love during a period of dating and engagement. If we examine the covenants of Ruth with Naomi (see Ruth 1: 1-17) and of David with Jonathan (see 1 Samuel 18:1-3), we find that the making of covenant vows came in relationships already bound by steadfast love and loyalty. A covenant, then, develops as partners grow in their commitment to each other over time; it is not just a public promise made to each other at the time of wedding.

C. Read Ruth's covenant with Naomi in Ruth 1:16-17. Write why you think this verse is often read or sung at wedding ceremonies.

_____

_____

The Israelites retold the stories of the Exodus and their developing relationship with God that led to the Sinai covenant. Retelling these stories celebrated their continuing covenant with God (see Deuteronomy 8:2; 11:2-7). In the same way, we need to remember and celebrate with each other the experiences that led to our growing commitment to a life together in covenant marriage.

D. Recall your growing commitment to your spouse over time by answering these questions.

What initially attracted you to your mate?

_____

When did you first feel you were in love?

_____

What were your thoughts and feelings on the day you became engaged?

_____

_____

For some, traditional wedding vows beautifully illustrate their covenant; others write their own vows to reflect the meaning of their commitment to each other. Whatever the vows, however, they cannot express the covenant between marital partners for all time. Even though Israel celebrated the events of covenant making during its wilderness wanderings, throughout the Bible Israel's understanding of God's steadfast loyalty developed and deepened. The

We need to remember and celebrate with each other the experiences that led to our growing commitment to a life together in covenant marriage

Sinai covenant was significant in the relationship between the chosen people and God, but the covenant relationship continued to grow and change. The high point of this developing covenant relationship between God and people is the new covenant, an outgrowth and the fulfillment of the covenant with God from the beginning (see Matthew 5:17).

As you look at your relationship before marriage and the reasons you committed yourselves to each other, changes may be evident to you. Your commitment and loyalty to each other look different now than they did then. Marriage covenants develop over time.

E. **Think back over your preconceptions about married life. Respond to each item below.**

One thing I said I'd never do:

_____

One thing I said I'd never say:

_____

One way I said I'd never change:

_____

F. The great Christian author C. S. Lewis wrote a book about his salvation titled *Surprised by Joy.* How has your spouse been a joyful surprise to you? List at least two ways your partner has shown loyalty and commitment to you that you might not have predicted on your wedding day.

1. _____

2. _____

Covenant partners take responsibility for their actions. James's brother was going into business for himself and needed some cash to get started. James trusted his brother and saw this as a golden opportunity to invest their savings for their son Billy's education for a much greater return than a banking account. Susan was reluctant; she did not trust her brother-in-law and did not think investing what they had worked so hard to save was wise. She did not want to disappoint James or anger him by questioning his judgment, however, so she agreed. James's brother went bankrupt, and Susan and James lost all their savings.

Who is responsible for what happened? Some of us want to blame James. Yet Susan chose not to voice her views, not to risk conflict, even if it brought the results that followed. She acted from loyalty and love for James; yet the results for both of them and their son were misfortune. James was responsible for his decision to invest, and Susan was responsible for her decision not to object. Neither can blame the other.

Covenant partners are responsible for what they do, even if what they do is

Marriage covenants develop over time

a living expression of their covenant with their partner. We see this principle even in the nonmarital covenant relationships in the Old Testament. Jonathan chose to defend his friend David to his father, Saul, who hated David. Yet Jonathan did not blame David for Saul's angry, violent response (see 1 Samuel 20:30-34). On the deaths of their husbands, Ruth chose to go with Naomi, even when Naomi decided to leave the land of Ruth's family. Together they lived in poverty, but Ruth did not blame Naomi for taking her to a foreign land or even for having to work in the fields from sunup to sundown to find enough grain to feed them both (see Ruth 2:7). There is no place in a covenant relationship for blaming partners for our own behavior, even if we choose to do what we do from love for and loyalty to our partner.

G. Check the blaming statements you have made to your spouse. Can you think of another one you use?
❑ If you were more sensitive, I wouldn't act this way!
❑ If you hadn't interfered, I would have worked it out!
❑ If you had insisted, I would have done it!
❑ Other:

_____

H. Read the following case study. John was installing new carpet in the bedroom and asked his wife to bring him some coffee. When she walked in, she tripped and spilled coffee on the new carpet. Check your response if you were John in this situation.
❑ Ask your wife why she did that and then criticize her for being clumsy.
❑ Let her know she's still OK and help her clean up the spill.
❑ Express your irritation first and then tell her you appreciate her willingness to help.
❑ Other:

_____

Check your response if you were the wife.
❑ **Run from the room in tears.**
❑ **Chuckle at your goof and clean up the mess.**
❑ **Apologize to John and try to do something special for him later.**
❑ Other:

_____

Covenants are based on freedom of choice. When we look at biblical covenants between persons, it is clear that no one was ever forced to act in certain ways by his or her covenant partner. In fact, in the covenant accounts the one who shows the steadfast loyalty of covenant love is usually in some position of being able to help the partner in a time of need. The acting partner is never a subordinate following the orders of a more powerful partner. David asked for Jonathan's support at a time when David was powerless in the face of Saul's wrath (see 1 Samuel 20:1-17). Ruth could have gone home; she had the same choices as her sister-in-law, Orphah (see Ruth 1:8-14). In the same way, God never forces us to act out our covenant commitment to God but leaves us free to choose even if it means failing.

There is no place in covenant marriage for one partner to force the other to

There is no place in a covenant relationship for blaming partners for our own behavior

be or do or think certain ways. We can ask, we can express our needs, but our covenant should not be used to club the other into submission to what we think is best. Submission is freely given to each other, not forced by one on the other (see Eph. 5:21). Submission grows from respect, not fear and manipulation.

I. **Read Ephesians 5:21. Check the paraphrase you think best states the truth of this passage.**
   ❏ Give in to your mate's wants and needs.
   ❏ Defer to your mate's best interests.
   ❏ Take turns with your mate being in charge.
   ❏ Bring yourself in line with God's intention for you and your mate.

Few spouses would not say, "But I don't try to force my partner into submission!" Yet when we try to manipulate our partners to change, to limit their options, that is exactly what we are doing. Wife wants Husband to spend more time together talking and sharing interests. She does not express her need directly but expresses only an interest in sexual intimacy if he has met her standards of conversational intimacy.

Of course, no marriage is perfect, and every spouse wants and needs the partner to make changes at times in their life together so that the relationship can deepen in its commitment. There is nothing wrong with asking for what we need or want from each other. Limiting or forcing the partner, though, are not appropriate change strategies for covenant relationships. Lesson 8 will focus on ways to approach change that respect rather than limit the freedom of covenant partners.

J. **Motivation is helping someone achieve mutually desirable goals. Manipulation is using someone else to achieve personal goals. Can you think of an incident in which you helped motivate your spouse to achieve mutual goals?**

The goal: _____

Your motivation: _____

Can you think of an incident in which you manipulated your spouse to achieve your own goals?

The goal: _____

Your manipulation: _____

Covenants are rooted in actions, not feelings. Most marriages began with the rapid heartbeat, constant thinking of the other, and difficulty focusing on anything except the other. We called it love. Feelings, however, wax and wane. A time comes when we no longer want to be in each other's company all the time, when the little quirks that used to be cute are now irksome, and when we don't feel overcome with joy each time our partner speaks. Rough spots inevitably come when we stick together even though we do not feel like it.

Covenant love is not those early exhilarating feelings or even later moments of newfound joy in our relationship. Certainly it does not mean interacting with

Rough spots inevitably come when we stick together even though we do not feel like it

our partner based on our feelings of the moment. Did Ruth feel like leaving her homeland and family? Did Jonathan feel like incurring his violent father's wrath?

Covenant suggests faithfulness in action. Scripture tells us to love our neighbor, who include our spouse, as ourselves. This is impossible if we define *love* only in terms of feeling. We cannot will the bodily changes we experience as feelings. What we can will is our behavior. We can choose what we will do, although we cannot choose how to feel. Jesus told us that there is no greater love than dying for the other (see John 15:13-14). Who feels like doing that?

Covenant love, then, involves a free decision to act in steadfast loyalty to each other. Yet this does not mean to grit your teeth and stick it out. It does not mean "I'll stay with you no matter what you do." Commitment out of obligation cannot be confused with covenant love.

What do we do, then, when we no longer feel loving toward our partner? Even though feelings are not the basis of covenant marriage, they are important gauges of the problems, needs, and strengths of our relationship with each other. A young couple with a new baby, an ill and demanding parent, and two careers need to pay attention to their feelings of loneliness and frustration with their growing distance from each other. Like gauges on our car's dashboard, feelings can tell us when we need to do preventive maintenance, when we need to refuel, and when we may have a serious problem. But few of us sell our cars because we need gas or the car overheats.

K. Label each incident *S* if it is the symptom of a problem that needs to be addressed or *F* if it represents temporary feelings that will change with time.
   ___ Jenny is furious when Ralph is late for dinner for the third night in a row.
   ___ Ralph resents Jenny's constant attention to their two-year-old.
   ___ Ralph gets angry when Jenny leaves her bike parked behind his car.

God's feelings with Israel were often anger and frustration (for example, see Numbers 11:1,10). God did not dismiss these feelings, nor did He abandon Israel. Instead, God called for needed change. The foundation of covenant, then, is loyalty, commitment; feelings can alert us to our covenant's developmental progress or difficulties that need attention. We need to use our feelings in behalf of our covenant instead of letting them define our covenant.

Part of the celebration of our covenant with each other needs to be remembering the rough spots when we stuck together and worked through problems despite one or both of us feeling like giving up. A more helpful approach is to focus on our partner's steadfast love and loyalty instead of our own, to avoid clubbing each other with "Look at the sacrifices I made for you."

L. Spend time thinking about ways your partner has responded to you from covenant love, even when he or she may not have felt like it. Use these suggestions or ones of your own.
   • When you were sick
   • When you disagreed on a course of action
   • When you had been particularly busy and preoccupied
   • When your spouse placed your needs above his or her own

We need to use our feelings in behalf of our covenant instead of letting them define our covenant

22

Describe one of those ways.

_____

_____

Covenant partners nurture their relationship. Covenant marriage is at times misunderstood as a license to sin against our partner, taking for granted our partner's commitment: "I know I was wrong to hurt you, but you vowed to stay with me for better or worse!" But in no biblical covenant does one partner take the other for granted. No biblical covenant partner ever called on the covenant as the reason the partner should forgive him. The covenant is not a safety net that keeps the marriage from crashing.

The "big" marital sin of infidelity is usually not what drains a marriage but the everyday taking each other for granted. We are less polite to our spouse than to the people with whom we work, and we are more likely to take out our accumulated frustrations in grumpiness on our partner than on our friends. We assume forgiveness for the little everyday slights that are part of living together. There is a good reason for this. We feel "safe" with our spouse. If we acted the same way with friends and colleagues, we might be labeled uncouth, unfriendly, a pain in the neck. We might find people pulling away from us. Although taking our spouse for granted is natural, it does not build the relationship.

M. Is it possible that you take your spouse for granted? Try this experiment for 24 hours. Keep a record of polite and impolite conversation on your part with your mate. On a sheet of paper make two columns. Label the left column *Polite* and the right column *Impolite.* Either write specific words used under the appropriate heading or make a mark indicating a response under the correct heading.

Covenant marriage grows as we care for each other, not take each other for granted. In the biblical covenants between persons, we see the covenants take on life as one partner cared for the other's need. For example, David needed Jonathan's protection. Spouses must ask each other for what they need from each other; it is in the asking and meeting of needs that the covenant grows and deepens.

Covenants are based on commitment freely offered. "I'll do this if you promise to ..." or "I've given and given, and you've done nothing" is not the way to begin a covenant relationship. Even Rahab, after risking her neck, did not say to the Israelite spies, "I've done all this for you, so you have to take care of me when the invasion comes." She simply asked them for what she needed, just as she had met their desperate need. Both expect the commitment of the other, but they do not keep score. Ruth did not expect Naomi to repay her for her loyalty and support (see Ruth 2:7).

In short, a covenant is not a contract. A covenant is a commitment of two persons to act in steadfast love to each other no matter what the consequences or payoff. Unfortunately, marriage is often reduced to a contract.

N. How do you know if you have been keeping a "scorecard" in your marriage? Generally, if you feel that you are the one who goes the second mile,

Covenant marriage grows as we care for each other, not take each other for granted

23

has more responsibilities, gets "dumped on," and goes unappreciated, you've been keeping score. One way to change this pattern is to consciously look for ways your spouse tries to meet your needs. Begin by listing five contributions your mate makes to your daily life.

1. _____

2. _____

3. _____

4. _____

5. _____

THE DIFFERENCE BETWEEN COVENANT AND CONTRACT

Contract is a more familiar idea to us than covenant. We have all signed contracts at one time or another, specifying what we will do for an employer, for example, in return for a certain wage. Legally, marriage is a contract, with certain rights and responsibilities. For this reason we cannot confuse legal marriage and covenant marriage. Legal marriage is a contract between two persons that can be ended in divorce if one party does not live up to his or her end of the bargain. Covenant marriage is an open-ended commitment to act lovingly and loyally without any conditions. Contracts are based on "if ... then" relationships: if you love me, then I will love you; if you are faithful to me, then I will be faithful to you; if you communicate openly with me, then I will be sexually open to you.

A contract cannot be the basis of a covenant relationship. That does not mean, however, that contracts have no place in covenants. God made a contract with Israel: " 'If you will diligently hearken to the voice of the Lord your God, and do that which is right in His eyes, and give heed to His commandments and keep all God's statutes, I will put none of the diseases upon you which I put upon the Egyptians; for I am the Lord, your healer' " (Exodus 15:26, RSV). But this contract was not the covenant. The relationship would not end if Israel failed to live up to the agreement. Many times, in fact, Israel did not meet its covenant responsibilities, but God kept the covenant (see Deuteronomy 7:9; 9:6).

Contracts, then, can be instruments to live life together. Working out agreements such as "I'll do the laundry if you'll take care of the kitchen cleanup" can ease many couples through the treacherous waters of household role assignments. "If you'll take care of the baby from 5:00 until 5:30 while I jog, I'll clean up the kitchen so that you can have some time to be alone" is the kind of contract that can inject sanity and order into what can often be chaotic and stressful lives.

Covenant partners will find these basic guidelines helpful in using contracts to build their relationship with each other.

Don't mistake the contract for the covenant. Contracts need to be focused on helping us grow and deepen our relationship and resolve difficulties; the relationship itself cannot be negotiated. Our love, affection, support, and loyalty are not items to be used as rewards for a partner's good behavior. To use our

Our love, affection, support, and loyalty are not items to be used as rewards for a partner's good behavior

steadfast love as a bargaining chip denies our covenant relationship. Contracts such as "I will not leave you if you ..." are not a part of covenant marriage.

Contract for positive change. When you make a contract with your partner, it needs to reflect something new in the relationship that you need or want, not something old that you want to get rid of. For example, "I want you to spend one evening a week with me," not "I want you to stop working so much." The focus, then, is on the possibility of positive change, not on problems.

Contract for specific actions. A contract also needs to specify exactly what you want your partner to say or do, not an attitude or general change in actions. For example, "I want you to talk with me at supper about your day and let me tell you about mine instead of watching the news," not "I want you to enjoy being with me more" or "I want you to pay attention to me more."

Make sure both partners offer something new and positive. The partner asking for change also needs to offer a new and positive behavior as part of the bargain. The other side of any of the requests in the above paragraphs needs to be a behavior that your partner would like from you that is new: "... and I'll help you clean up after supper," "... and I'll plan an evening of fun and relaxation so that you can go back to work refreshed" are appropriate other sides to those contracts, not "... or I'll stop doing the washing," "... or I'm going to make you wish you had." Contracts should always be opportunities for both partners to get icing on the cake they already have, not threats of losing the fulfillment they now provide each other.

O. Rephrase the following contracts to make them specific and positive.

I want you to be more responsible with our money.

_____

_____

I want you to help me around the house more.

_____

_____

Contracts should be considered time-limited experiments, not permanent amendments. Contracts offer partners a chance to try out new ways of relating to each other. When they work, these new ways of relating may become part of their life together. When developing a contract with each other, set a time limit (a week, a month) when the experience will be evaluated. James and Susan may find that discussing their days over dinner without the television on and sharing dinner cleanup have become important ways of relating to one another that they want to be an ongoing part of their life together. Sharing cleanup no longer depends on dinner conversation.

P. Practice developing a contract with your spouse. Write one small behavior change you would like from him or her and one change you are willing to make in return. Fill in the contract on the next page and sign it.

Contracts offer partners a chance to try out new ways of relating to each other

If you will _____ ,

then I will _____

for one week, beginning_____.

Signed _____

Consider sharing your contract with your spouse at the next group session.

KEEPING CONTRACTS IN THEIR PLACE

Contracts offer the possibilities of creative change in marriage. However, they need to be kept in their place. Contracts are in many ways games we agree to play with each other; the danger is letting them become the only way we relate to each other. This is the danger of creeping contractuality. Asking ourselves the following questions are symptoms of creeping contractuality: *Am I getting what I deserve from this marriage? Could I get a better deal investing elsewhere (an affair, another marriage, throwing myself into my work or parenting or friendships)? Can I force my partner to meet my expectations?*

When we answer yes to any of these questions, we need to renew our covenant with our mate. This requires a conscious decision to commit ourselves with steadfast love to each other without qualification, asking both God's witness to our covenant and God's guidance in constant prayer. It then requires action, implementing the six principles of covenant marriage in our daily walk together.

In beginning or renewing a covenant marriage, partners must make a conscious commitment to steadfast love without qualification

SUMMARY

Marriage can be a covenant relationship in ways similar to the divine-human covenant between God and Israel and like the human-human covenant relationships between persons in the Bible. Just as God's covenant with Israel was based on steadfast love, marriage partners covenant to act in steadfast love and unconditional loyalty to each other. This relationship of commitment grows and develops over time. A covenant is not a contract, although contracts can be useful in managing covenant relationships. In beginning or renewing a covenant marriage, partners must make a conscious commitment to steadfast love without qualification. They must then live the six principles of covenant marriage in their daily walk together.

CHECKPOINT

The following review exercise is designed to reveal whether you have achieved the learning goals for lesson 1. Answer each question. Correct answers are given after the final question.

1. Label each statement below with *cov* for *covenant* or *con* for *contract.*
   ___ a. Is legally binding
   ___ b. Is open-minded without conditions
   ___ c. The relationship cannot be negotiated
   ___ d. Has certain rights and responsibilities
   ___ e. Is based on steadfast love and loyalty

2. Fill in the blanks to complete each of the six characteristics of a covenant relationship.
   a. Covenants are the fruit of a _____, _____ relationship.
   b. Covenant partners take _____ for their _____.
   c. Covenants are based on _____ of choice.
   d. Covenants are rooted in _____, not _____.
   e. Covenant partners _____ their _____.
   f. Covenants are based on _____ freely offered.
3. Mark the following *T* for *true* or *F* for *false*. A marriage covenant is like God's covenant with His people because—
   ___ a. it is based on steadfast love;
   ___ b. it is a partnership of equals;
   ___ c. it includes contracts but goes beyond them;
   ___ d. it can be broken by both parties;
   ___ e. it develops over a period of time.
4. Review the covenant with your spouse that you wrote in the introductory session. Are there changes you would like to make in your covenant, based on new understandings from lesson 1? Make these changes below.

_____

_____

_____

Now check your answers.
1. a. *con,* b. *cov,* c. *cov,* d. *con,* e. *cov*
2. a. loving, faithful; b. responsibility, actions; c. freedom; d. actions, feelings; e. nurture, relationship; f. commitment
3. a. *T,* b. *F* (Persons are not equal to God; yet individuals in marriage are equal), c. *T,* d. *F,* e. *T*
4. Personal response

LOOKING AHEAD

How is a marriage modeled on God's covenant love a picture of His love for us? In lesson 2 we will examine God's covenant with those He loves in order to gain guidance for living the covenant of marriage. We will ask ourselves: *What will it cost me to be in covenant with my marriage partner? What will I gain if I commit myself to a covenant marriage?*

MARRIAGE AS PROMISE

Lesson 2

The only way a marriage relationship can demonstrate God's relationship with us is if marriage truly mirrors in some way Christ's love for us

LOOKING BACK

In lesson 1 we examined the biblical concept of covenant particularly as it applied to the covenant between persons in the Old Testament. We discovered six characteristics of covenant relationships. Can you name them?

Recall the covenant you and your spouse entered. How has it affected your daily life this past week? What implications does it have for new ways of relating to each other in the future?

OVERVIEW

Lesson 2 continues our look at biblically based covenant relationships, focusing on God's promises. What are the promises of a marriage based on God's covenant love? What does it cost to be involved in a covenant relationship?

In this lesson you will identify some of the benefits to be found in relating to your partner with love, loyalty, and grace. When you complete this lesson, you will be able to—

- describe the potential of a covenant marriage;
- identify five qualities of a covenant marriage based on biblical teachings;
- evaluate your marriage based on the qualities of a covenant marriage;
- identify three ways your marriage can move toward the potential of a covenant marriage;
- take steps to achieve a covenant marriage.

QUALITIES OF A COVENANT MARRIAGE

When Old and New Testament writers wanted to describe God's love for people, they often used the picture of a marriage relationship. For example, in Ephesians 5:21-33 Paul used the relationship between husband and wife to picture Christ's love for and relationship with the church.

The only way a marriage relationship can demonstrate God's relationship with us, however, is if marriage truly mirrors in some way Christ's love for us. It is not just any marriage, then, but a marriage modeled on God's covenant love that can in turn be a picture of God's love. To understand covenant marriage, we need to look not only at the covenant relationships between persons, as we did in the previous lesson, but also at God's covenant promises.

Examining God's covenant with those He loves, then, can give us guidance

28

for living in the covenant of marriage. What are some qualities of a covenant marriage modeled on God's covenant love?

Covenant marriage is permanent. God's love "never ceases" (Lamentations 3:22, RSV); nothing will "be able to separate us from the love of God" (Romans 8:38-39). God's love is patient and enduring, even through hurt and disappointment. In the same way, marriage is a permanent relationship, like a single body that cannot be divided, "one flesh" (Ephesians 5:31). The essence of a covenant, unlike a contract, is that it is unconditional. There are no legal responsibilities that, when not fulfilled, end the relationship.

Isn't this a cruel word for those who have already suffered through the hurt of a divorce? Where is the recognition of our limitations, our imperfection, our sinfulness? Did Jesus mean when He said, "What therefore God hath joined together, let not man put asunder" (Mark 10:9; Matthew 19:6) that people should continue living in relationships that are destroying them as individuals? Two issues are involved that can help us respond to these serious questions.

First, emotionally and interpersonally, relationships cannot end. We can stop living together, stop talking to each other, and stop seeing each other, but the other is nevertheless a part of who we are because of our history together. For some, the relationships in parenting and with extended family almost require continuing a relationship with each other even in the aftermath of divorce.

A friend went through a painful separation and divorce after 20 years of marriage. He tried to remove every trace of the marriage from his life. With great ritual he stood one evening with the years of accumulated photographs from family vacations, throwing them one by one in the fire. Then the realization struck: to destroy everything that reminded him of her was to destroy his own past; his roots; many good memories; and, in the end, his own identity. His ways of relating to others, his ideas, even his habits, such as which side of the bed to sleep on, had all been shaped by his marriage with her. Even if he never saw or spoke with her again, she had been and was always part of his life.

Second, however, it is important to remember that we are talking about covenant marriage, and not all marriages are based on the steadfast love and unconditional loyalty of a covenant modeled on God's love for people. Covenant marriage happens when two persons have made a commitment to Jesus Christ and to each other. Covenant marriage means living in loyalty modeled on such a commitment as Jesus demonstrated when He gave Himself for the church. Permanence, then, is not adequate to describe the limitless loyalty of a covenant relationship. The permanence of marriage is not only a statement of fact, then, but also an ideal.

In the previous lesson we mentioned that the wedding-day vows are not the covenant but a public and legal announcement of a covenant that has already been established and will continue to develop and deepen. Weddings are not covenants. In the same way, a divorce is really a death certificate, a public and legal announcement of a covenant already broken. It is important that we do not confuse legal divorce with breaking a covenant. A warning is here even for couples who would never consider divorce an option. We can compromise our covenant with each other or reduce it to a contract; we can remain legally married but spiritually in a process of divorce. We can live together in legal marriage, sinning all the while against the marriage covenant in which we promised to give of ourselves loyally and steadfastly.

Covenant marriage means living in loyalty modeled on such a commitment as Jesus demonstrated when He gave Himself for the church

A. Write ways we can sin against our marriage covenant while remaining legally married.

_____

_____

Covenant marriage costs. By entering a covenant with God, Israel gave up other gods and followed Yahweh to wander in the wilderness. Certainly, the Israelites were not shy about letting Moses and Yahweh know that they had given up bountiful tables in Egypt for the uncertainties of the wilderness (see Exodus 16:2-3).

The marriage covenant, too, costs us the life we know as we take the risk of committing ourselves to live loyally and lovingly together in a future we do not yet know. The Bible identifies the condition of the one-flesh relationship as leaving behind father and mother (see Ephesians 5:31). What does this mean? It is not as though we were 19th-century pioneers, striking off in a covered wagon westward, knowing that we will never see our families again. Most of us continue to have important relationships with our parents and other family. But we no longer center our life in the family we grew up in. For better or worse, we choose to face the future and its uncertainties with this covenant partner.

For better or worse, we choose to face the future and its uncertainties with this covenant partner

B. Have you left father and mother behind emotionally in favor of your marriage partner? ❑ Yes ❑ No If not, what do you need to do in order to make the break with your parents?

_____

_____

We not only leave our parents behind in the ongoing relationship of covenant marriage but also choose paths together at the cost of other choices. Perhaps, like Ruth in her covenant with Naomi, it requires a move to a new and unfamiliar place. Even if we remain in the same neighborhood we grew up in, however, we must work out a lifestyle and make choices different from those we might have made if we had only ourselves to think about. Dual-career couples know full well that career opportunities must sometimes be declined because of our commitment to each other. Every aspect of life bears the mark of our choice.

Covenant marriage is both freedom and obligation. The Jewish people had difficulty recognizing that even though God had entered a covenant with them, He did not owe them. Jesus made this clear when some were flaunting their specialness in God's eyes; God could raise up a covenant people out of the stones of the earth (see Luke 3:8). God chooses to live the covenant; no contract forces covenant partners to be steadfastly loyal and loving.

When we start trying to force a partner to be loyal, to be loving, we have sinned against our covenant relationship. Instead of focusing on our own responsibilities and commitments, we are trying to get the splinter out of our spouse's eye. When we turn our attention to what we ought to be getting from our partner, we have turned the relationship into a contract, saying, "My chief concern is my rights, what I am due, not what I can give."

C. **What have you tried to get your partner to do for you that he or she has persistently refused or failed to do?**

_____

Do you have the right to expect your mate to comply with your request?
❑ Yes ❑ No

How would giving your mate the freedom to fail to meet your expectations in this area affect your relationship with each other?

_____

_____

Even so, obligations exist in a covenant marriage. The paradox of God's free grace, paired with the expectation of fruitful Christian living, carries over into marriage. Because covenant partners are free does not mean that we can do what we please but that we can choose how to act from love and loyalty to our partner. Basic expectations exist in every marriage, such as fidelity and companionship, that we choose to make a part of our covenant with each other.

Some of the choices we make in our marriage covenant differ from those others choose because they reflect our commitment to meet each other's needs. John grew up with parents who never talked about their problems, but John remembered the long, cold silences between them. He remembered not being able to eat because the quiet was so oppressive and trying to stay away from the thick silence by playing alone in his room. When Beverly married John, she soon learned how painful silent anger was for him. Part of their covenant with one another was to voice their anger, even if they could not always work through the problems at the time.

D. **Write an example of a role expectation you had of your mate based on your parents' relationship with each other. For example, did you expect that the husband would carry out the trash because your father always carried out the trash?**

_____

_____

Each of us has obligations we have chosen to make to each other. Often these obligations are unspoken agreements about needs and ways we can care for each other. In celebrating our covenant with each other, it is helpful to recall ways our partner has committed himself or herself to us that have special meaning.

Because covenant partners are free does not mean that we can do what we please but that we can choose how to act from love and loyalty to our partner

E. How has your partner lived in covenant with you by taking on certain obligations with a loving spirit? Examples: never talking about your disagreements to friends behind your back or sacrificing financially so that you could get your teeth straightened.

_____

_____

Covenant marriage is defined by the partners, not by others' expectations. Perhaps one of Jesus' most shocking acts was to call God Abba, which means Daddy. Throughout His ministry the message was clear that God is a personal God. No special rules exist for how we are to relate to God; we are not limited by ritual washing and to special places reserved for worship. Instead, we are to pray without ceasing and to ask God for whatever we need. Ours is not a legalistic relationship with a God in the highest heaven we can approach only through elaborate ritual.

In the same way, covenant marriage is a personal relationship, not a set of rules that have to be lived. Covenant marriage is not defined by lines of authority and specific role expectations. How we are to relate to each other is defined not by rules about what is appropriate behavior for males and females but by our gifts and needs.

F. Place each of the following responsibilities under the heading you consider appropriate: child care, doing dishes, housecleaning, paying bills, taking out trash, handling investments, yard work, taking kids to the doctor.

Husband	Wife	Both

Listening to each other is the key to a covenant relationship

The people of God often lost the importance of relationship with God, focusing instead on rules and expectations about how to meet their end of the covenant relationship. The Lord made it clear that in the beginning, the covenant meant fellowship and devotion of Israel and the Lord to each other. The people, however, broke the covenant with all of their laws and rites and ceremonies about the right ways to worship God. The people stopped listening to God (see Jeremiah 7:21-26).

Listening to each other, then, is the key to a covenant relationship. To meet each other's needs, we must know them, and how can we know if we do not listen? Every husband is different from every other husband. Every wife is different from every other wife. Our needs and gifts differ. We begin marriage with our own picture about the ways husbands and wives "ought" to relate to each other, perhaps from our parents' marriage or even marriages we see on television. But if it is truly a covenant in which we commit ourselves to caring for one another, we quickly learn that our marriage cannot follow someone else's blueprint.

G. Write ways your marriage differs from that of your parents in terms of—
lines of authority:

_____

_____

tasks and responsibilities:

_____

_____

Covenant marriage is intentional. As we read through the Old and New Testaments, we see God's purposes unfolding through history. God's covenant with Israel was to be a means of redemption for all nations. God's covenant with the church calls us to bear fruit in our ministry in the world. Covenant relationships, then, have purposes. They are intended not only to provide fellowship between covenant partners but also to bear fruit in the world.

Fruitful relationships are growing relationships. A covenant marriage has direction. We are always headed toward making our relationship a witness to our Lord's grace and love. In covenant marriage our aim is to demonstrate the transforming power of God's love in human relationships. It is, therefore, a never-ending journey.

H. Complete a marriage time line by indicating highs and lows of your life together. Begin with dating and continue to the present. Here is an example:

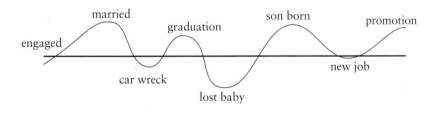

Now complete your marriage time line:

_____

Most of us would not be reading this if we had not recognized the significance of our marriage in our covenant with God. We need a chance to look at where we have been and where we need to go in deepening and strengthening our covenant with each other. Sins against each other and storms from the outside that rock our relationship are inevitable. Through it all, however,

In covenant marriage our aim is to demonstrate the transforming power of God's love in human relationships. It is a never-ending journey

covenant marriage is founded on grace—the promise of steadfast loyalty as we once again find our way together.

I. How does your marriage compare to a covenant marriage characterized by these five qualities? Circle the number corresponding to your answer.
1 = exceptional, 2 = satisfactory, 3 = needs improvement.

Covenant marriage is permanent.	1 2 3
Covenant marriage costs.	1 2 3
Covenant marriage is both freedom and obligation.	1 2 3
Covenant marriage is relational.	1 2 3
Covenant marriage is intentional.	1 2 3

Total _____

If you scored less than 10 points, you are doing well in achieving a covenant marriage.

Up to this point, covenant marriage has seemed an awesome commitment, and it is. Yet it is also helpful to examine the promised fruits of living in covenant with each other.

PROMISES OF A COVENANT MARRIAGE

Unconditional Love

Covenant partners are family to each other; they belong to each other no matter what. Paul said it beautifully: "Love never fails" (1 Corinthians 13:8, NASB). This does not mean that we can do what we please and take the partner's unconditional acceptance for granted. But the relationship will not end because we are less than perfect and less than we can be.

J. Read 1 Corinthians 13:4-7. List the phrases describing what love is and what love is not.

Love Is ...   Love Is Not ...

_____   _____

_____   _____

_____   _____

_____   _____

Forgiveness

A part of unconditional love is the process of forgiveness. Forgiveness allows us to move past hurts and failures to a strengthened covenant with each other. It is one way we show evidence of God's love for us (see Ephesians 4:32).

The relationship will not end because we are less than perfect and less than we can be

K. Check each statement that you would agree with or that would characterize you.

❏ When I am hurt, I want to hurt back.

❏ I forgive, but I have to be mad for a while first.

❏ I forgive if my partner promises not to do it again.

❏ When I forgive my partner, I expect him or her to make it up to me.

❏ In order to really forgive, I need to forget the whole incident.

Here are the characteristics of forgiveness in covenant marriage.

Forgiveness focuses on restoring the relationship, not getting even (see Matthew 5:38-39; Romans 12:17-21; 1 Peter 3:9-12). Our first reaction when we are hurt by our partner is to hurt back. The impulse to defend ourselves is natural. The need to communicate our hurt and anger to our partner is important. But in the end neither of these purposes is accomplished by hurting our partner. Since covenant marriage is a one-flesh relationship, to hurt your partner is to hurt yourself. By striking back, we widen the gulf of hurt and anger between us rather than find ways to heal the relationship. Of course, we need to communicate our hurt or anger, but to do so by hurting or angering the partner puts the partner on the defensive rather than helps us look together at the rift between us.

Forgiveness is offered freely, not as a contract. Forgiveness does not depend on the partner's making amends or swearing never to do it again. "I'll forgive you and forget the whole thing ever happened if you promise never to throw anything away that belongs to me" is not forgiveness; it is striking a deal.

Forgiveness holds each responsible for his or her behavior. Forgiveness may be free, but it is not cheap. It does not excuse or tolerate broken promises and breaches of covenant. God does not wink at our sin; we are responsible for what we do. In the same way, partners in covenant marriage hold each other responsible for what he or she does.

Several times in the past month Walter has been coming home hours late from work without calling Susan. She just learned that he has bought a new car without consulting her and has agreed to transfer to a distant city, where his responsibilities will be even greater. Always before, they have made decisions together. What should Susan do? She knows that he has been under a lot of pressure; perhaps his decision making without her could not be helped. Or perhaps this is the way men in his position are supposed to behave; she will just have to learn to live with it.

With either of these responses Susan has denied Walter's responsibility for himself, looking at his behavior either as unavoidable or out of his control. What would happen if Susan shared her feelings with Walter? They would have a chance to talk about their relationship, their commitment to each other, and whether they are satisfied with the shape their lives are taking. She may then forgive him. But there can be forgiveness only if partners recognize that their mates are responsible for what they do.

Forgiveness is one step in the process of restoring a relationship, but it must be met by confession and change. What if Susan confronts Walter with her feelings, and his response is "So what?" She has held him responsible for his choices, but there is still a breach in the covenant. Susan may forgive him, but her forgiveness alone cannot bridge the gap between them. A covenant must be mutual; one can hold out the opportunity for covenant renewal through

There can be forgiveness only if partners recognize that their mates are responsible for what they do

forgiveness, but the other is always free to reject the offer. Only through confession and turning toward restoring the relationship can the covenant relationship grow and deepen from the trials of hurt and sin. Forgiveness frees our partner from trying to make it up to us (a contract concept). It enables us to work together to learn and grow from our troubles. But it does not ensure a restored relationship.

Forgiveness is not forgetting but, by remembering, celebrates the future. To forget what is forgiven is to throw away the fruits of the covenant relationship. Our victory over the sin in our life together gives us cause to celebrate. Remembering the trials in our relationship, like the Israelites' retelling the story of God's faithfulness through their sinfulness, gives us hope for the future.

L. Reread your answers to exercise K. Which one(s) do you need to change in order to become a more forgiving person?

Comfort

A third promise of covenant marriage is the comfort of our partner. Our covenant promises that we will care for each other, share in the hurts and joys of life, and provide a safe harbor for each other when we are battered by the world. How can we be good comforters for each other?

A comforter listens. Like the Great Comforter, who hears even our inward groanings, a comforter tunes in not only to the words but also to the partner's feelings and unspoken thoughts. When we truly comfort each other, we try with our total being to understand what the other is experiencing. "I know just how you feel. Just last week the same thing happened to me. Let me tell you about it" is not comforting. This response turns the focus onto the listener and away from the partner needing comfort. To be truly comforting, partners must focus on their mate, not on themselves and their experiences.

A comforter does not say, "I told you so." We have all experienced the cold and uncomfort of someone else's "I told you so." Why then are we quick to say it?

Perhaps there is no more helpless feeling than watching someone I love, my covenant partner, feeling sad or hurt. I want to *do* something to make it better. As helpful as listening is to the hurt partner, as a comforter I feel helpless and powerless to change a painful situation. "I told you so," however, restores my sense of power. I *can* protect my partner from hurt. All he or she has to do is listen to me the next time!

In many ways, "I told you so" can be a misguided expression of love. However, it is heard as judgment, not comfort.

A comforter offers advice or intervenes only when invited. Much like "I told you so," offering advice or jumping into the situation ourselves is often another way of trying to feel less helpless in the face of our partner's pain.

When Phil told Sarah about the difficulties he was having at the office, her response was something like "How could he say such a thing! He should know how grateful he ought to be to you. You march right in there tomorrow and tell him off! I think you ought to quit and find a job where you are appreciated." At a later time she threatened to call and give Phil's colleagues a piece of her mind. She could not bear to listen to his troubles because she found it so difficult not to be able to make the situation better for him in some

Our covenant promises that we will care for each other, share in the hurts and joys of life, and provide a safe harbor for each other when we are battered by the world

way. Phil ended up soothing Sarah instead of finding comfort from sharing with her. He finally stopped telling her about things that worried or upset him.

Offering advice or intervening without being asked takes away our partner's freedom and responsibility for self, both necessary ingredients in covenant marriage.

M. Check the statements that offer comfort.
❏ I had an experience like that once, but it worked out fine.
❏ Next time don't buy gas there.
❏ I think you should be mad. Give them a piece of your mind.
❏ I'm really sorry that happened. You must have felt awful.
❏ I wish I could do something to help. But know that I care.

Hope

Finally, covenant marriage holds the promise of hope. There are three bases for hope in covenant marriage.

Our covenant focuses on victories in our relationship together. We have weathered storms and experienced grace and forgiveness. Remembering and celebrating have important places in our covenant relationship; present tribulations are seen in the context of our ongoing covenant and our history of steadfast loyalty.

Our covenant focuses on what we can do, not on what we can't. Perhaps we cannot stop the arms race or end poverty, but our relationship can make a difference in the lives of our children, our families, and our community. Our relationship is not just a way to get our own needs met but a witness to God's redeeming grace and promise of covenant with all humankind.

N. Biblical hope is not wishful thinking but eager anticipation of an expected outcome. Write what gives you hope in your marriage when you think about—

something you accomplished together in the past:

_____

_____

something you are working on together in the present:

_____

_____

Our covenant recognizes that we are part of the kingdom of God that is breaking into this world. God promises blessings of mercy and grace more than sufficient to overcome our weaknesses and sinfulness as marital partners. God is bigger than our problems and stands as a witness to our covenant with each other. What a promise!

> *Our relationship is not just a way to get our own needs met but a witness to God's redeeming grace and promise of covenant with all humankind*

O. List three ways your marriage can move toward the potential of a covenant marriage.

1. _____

2. _____

3. _____

P. Write one specific step you can take this week to move in the direction of achieving a covenant marriage.

_____

_____

SUMMARY

Through grace we find our way together as we deepen and strengthen our love

Although we may want to live in a covenant relationship with our partner, some qualities must be present in a marriage for it to reflect God's covenant love. Covenant marriage is permanent, costly, and intentional. Covenant marriage is both freedom and obligation. Covenant marriage is defined by the partners, not by others' expectations.

In covenant marriage our aim is to demonstrate the transforming power of God's love in human relationships. Through grace we find our way together as we deepen and strengthen our love.

The awesome commitment required of a covenant marriage is balanced by the promised fruits of living in covenant with each other. These outgrowths of commitment include unconditional love, forgiveness, comfort, and hope.

CHECKPOINT

The following review exercise is designed to reveal whether you have achieved the learning goals for lesson 2. Answer each question. Correct answers are given after the final question.

1. Recall the qualities of a covenant marriage by filling in the blanks.
   a. Covenant marriage is _____.
   b. Covenant marriage _____.
   c. Covenant marriage is both _____ and
      _____.
   d. Covenant marriage is defined by the _____, not by others' _____.
   e. Covenant marriage is _____.
2. Check four promises of a covenant marriage.
   ❑ love   ❑ hope   ❑ forgiveness
   ❑ happiness   ❑ security   ❑ fulfillment
   ❑ comfort   ❑ companionship   ❑ peace
3. Write *T* for *true* and *F* for *false*.
   ___ a. Forgiveness allows us to communicate our hurt and anger.
   ___ b. Forgiveness depends on the partner's promising never to do it again.

   ___ c. Forgiveness tolerates and excuses breaches of the covenant.
   ___ d. Forgiveness can be rejected by the erring partner.
   ___ e. Forgiveness frees the partner to respond with confession and change.
   ___ f. Forgiveness requires forgetting the injury.

4. Change the wording in the following incorrect statements to make them correct.

   a. A comforter tells his or her similar experience.

   _____

   b. A comforter says, "I told you so."

   _____

   c. A comforter always offers advice.

   _____

5. Check which of these five statements contain the three bases for hope in a covenant marriage.
   ❑ a. Remembering past victories we have shared
   ❑ b. Forgetting the past and looking only to the future
   ❑ c. Focusing on what we can do together
   ❑ d. Making a difference in world affairs
   ❑ e. Recognizing that we are part of God's kingdom

Now check your answers.
1. a. permanent; b. costs; c. freedom, obligation; d. partners, expectations, others; e. intentional
2. love, forgiveness, comfort, hope
3. a. *T,* b. *F,* c. *F,* d. *T,* e. *T,* f. *F*
4. a. A comforter listens. b. A comforter does not say, "I told you so." c. A comforter offers advice only when invited.
5. a, c, e

LOOKING AHEAD

In unit 2, "A Journey Inward," lesson 3 will focus on the uniqueness of each partner in the relationship. What are your unique gifts as a person? What are your partner's gifts? You will discover ways to implement and nurture both spouses' gifts as a means of strengthening your covenant relationship.

UNIT 2

A JOURNEY
INWARD

HONORING OUR UNIQUENESS
Lesson 3

In unit 1 we examined the benefits of marriage as a covenant relationship, based on the biblical model of covenant. We discovered the implications for new ways of relating to our spouse, based on the six characteristics of a covenant relationship. We were reminded of God's promises to persons who commit themselves to a marriage based on God's covenant love. These promised outgrowths of commitment include unconditional love, forgiveness, comfort, and hope.

OVERVIEW

Unit 2, "A Journey Inward," focuses on the covenant relationship as a means to enhance the strengths of each person in the marriage. Lesson 3 will enable you to identify and affirm the gifts you and your mate bring to your covenant partnership.

What does it mean to honor each other's uniqueness? How can we dishonor it by an emphasis on too much individuality or too much unity? How can we daily choose our partner as God's special gift?

When you complete this lesson, you will be able to—
- define what it means to be a person;
- recognize the wholeness of persons in relationship;
- assess and affirm your gifts as a person;
- identify and affirm your mate's gifts as a person;
- nurture your gifts and those of your mate.

OF ALL THE POSSIBILITIES, WE CHOSE EACH OTHER
Remember when you decided your spouse was really the one you wanted to marry? What was it about this person? Whatever it was, you recognized that in some way this was a special person, "the one for me."

A. Jot down one characteristic that initially attracted you to your spouse.

The Initial Covenant Choice
In many ways the choice to commit ourselves in marriage to each other resembles the choice we made to become a Christian. Some had a Damascus-

Remember when you decided your spouse was really the one you wanted to marry? What was it about this person?

41

road experience. Paul had actively hated the Christians until a personal encounter with the living Lord on the road to Damascus turned him around (see Acts 9:1-9). Some couples began their relationship actively disliking each other until some circumstance caused them to see each other with new eyes. They recognized in the other something special they had not seen before. Others heard bells and saw stars the first time they saw each other and immediately knew that this was the special one—it was love at first sight. Many couples, however, find their commitment to each other growing from a long period of relationship. The decision to marry may have seemed a natural development in their growing commitment. In later years they may even have difficulty agreeing exactly when they decided to marry.

B. Was your decision to marry—
   ❏ a sudden or relatively quick decision?
   ❏ the result of a long, growing relationship?

We are not always aware of the reasons we choose each other. There is a saying that love is blind, but couples choose each other for complex and important reasons, whether conscious or unconscious. Identifying the reasons we chose each other helps pinpoint the something special, the uniqueness of our partner. All of us come to marriage with an agenda; important values, hopes, and dreams for our lives; longings and needs we hope the other person can help us fill. You may want to reconstruct your own agenda for marrying your partner as a way to identify how you knew your partner was the one.

C. The following questions can help you identify parts of your marriage agenda. As you read each question, either answer it mentally or write your answer on a separate piece of paper.
   1. When you first met, did you and your partner have similar interests and enjoy the same activities?
   2. What were your dreams and goals for your life at the time you met and dated? Did you talk about these with each other? Were dreams and goals alike or different?
   3. How did you communicate with your partner? What did you talk about? Did you feel understood, that your partner was easy to talk to?
   4. In what ways was your partner unlike you? How did you feel about those differences?
   5. What weaknesses in yourself did you want to strengthen? How did your partner seem to be the kind of person who could help you with that?
   6. What characteristics of your parents' marriage stand out in your mind? In what ways did you want a partner who would help you create a relationship like your parents' marriage? Different from your parents' marriage?
   7. How did other people, like friends and family, feel about your partner? What effect did their feelings have on yours?
   8. What did you most want to avoid in marriage?

As you answered these questions, you probably realized that you knew a great deal about each other, even though you may not have thought much about your reasons for being attracted to each other at the time. Your goals and values interacted with those of your partner to influence each other and

> *All of us come to marriage with an agenda; important values, hopes, and dreams for our lives; longings and needs we hope the other person can help us fill*

push you toward the decision to marry. This other person was indeed unique and special.

Covenant Partners Keep On Choosing Each Other

As special as you were to each other in the beginning, the process of choosing each other above all others was not completed when you said, "I do." One of the most important characteristics of a covenant relationship is that choice making does not end at the time of covenant making. Covenant partners are steadfastly loyal to each other, but they also continue to be free to choose. In our daily lives we continue to choose our partner as the special one. As in the beginning, we may not even be aware of our process of choosing each other, of recognizing the other as the special one in our life. But we choose. We choose to confide in each other, to depend on each other, and to plan a future together. We choose to keep some parts of our thoughts and lives private and to share others. The choice is not only to remain married but also to choose *this* person to be my partner, whether in a game of tennis, a conversation about world affairs, or a problem. It is a continuing process of saying to ourselves, *I choose* _____.

D. Make a commitment to your mate as the marriage partner you choose for today and the future. Repeat the following statement aloud now, with God as your witness: I, _____, choose _____ as my covenant partner for today and for the rest of our days.

Some reasons you choose your partner each day are rooted in the beginning of your relationship. As you had hoped, your partner has been able to fulfill those initial needs and dreams. But needs and dreams also change, and we each change with them. What is special to you about your partner may have changed as you and your partner—and your marriage—have changed and grown over time. We occasionally need to remind each other about the stories of our courtship and how special we were to each other back then.

We also need to tell our partners why we still choose them above all others. There is no other person like your marriage partner! Ways your partner meets your needs today may or may not be the same as they were in the beginning. In what ways now is your partner special, different from all of the others?

E. As you read each question, answer it to yourself before going on to the next question.
   1. What attracts you to your partner today? What similar interests and activities do you share?
   2. What are some of the dreams and goals for your life now that you and your mate have shared with each other?
   3. Describe your communication with your spouse. When do you find it easiest to talk with her or him?
   4. In what ways is your partner different from you? How do you feel about those differences?
   5. What weaknesses in yourself would you like to strengthen? How does your partner help you be the kind of person you want to be?
   6. How has your marriage been like that of your parents? Different from your parents?

We need to tell our partners why we still choose them above all others. There is no other person like your marriage partner!

7. How have your friends and family affirmed your choice of a mate? How has their reaction affected your feelings about your mate?
8. Have you managed to avoid your worst fear about married life? Does that fear still threaten you as you look to your future together?

Important in a covenant marriage is the fact that partners affirm each other's uniqueness—the other's gifts and the ways the other is important. But to be special and unique to each other does not mean that covenant-marriage partners are totally wrapped up in each other, as perhaps we were during the early days of dating and marriage. You remember that time. We hung on every word the other said; we watched the other's eyes and actions for signs that confirmed our love for each other. All we wanted was to be alone together. Nothing else seemed important.

This may be the way courtship and marriage begin; but if over the years of marriage a couple continues to expect to be the whole world to each other, we may run into two problems.

Problem 1: We take personally every action and word of the partner. Carlos had been working at home the past few days on a presentation he was to make before the board of directors. By working at home, he hoped to escape the interruptions of the office. At 2:00, however, the termite inspector came. At 2:30 Matt's teacher called to say that seven-year-old Matt was running a fever. Carlos picked up Matt at school, ran by the pediatrician's office, picked up a prescription, and settled his son down at home with some books to read. After school hours the doorbell rang four times when neighborhood children wanted to find out why Matt could not play with them.

When Amelia arrived home at 5:30, she noticed that Carlos seemed distant and distracted. She fixed his favorite dinner while he worked a little longer. He hardly said a word during dinner, and Amelia wondered what was wrong.

After Matt had gone to sleep, Amelia bumped into Carlos in the hall as he was headed back to his study. She gave him a hug, but he brushed on by. Feeling stung, she asked: "Why are you so angry with me? What have I done?" Carlos's response was "I'm not angry; I've just got a lot to do." Amelia retorted: "Is it too much to ask for a five-second hug, to say thanks for a good dinner, to notice that I'm here? If you loved me, the least you could do is tell me why you are so angry with me." Carlos, in disgust, answered, "If you loved me, you would recognize how much pressure I'm under and support me instead of making it harder."

Both Carlos and Amelia took personally the other's words and actions. Both heard their partner saying, "I am unhappy with you." Both had needs that went unmet. Both felt a disturbance in the relationship and assumed that it must be the result of what one or the other had failed to do as a spouse.

The problem with taking personally all of our partner's behaviors is that our partners are responding to many other people and events besides ourselves. Frustrations at work, a project around the house that does not go as planned, fatigue, worry about children or an ailing parent, and many other factors can make a partner seem distant, angry, unhappy. The wife who bounces out of bed ready to greet each new dawn may feel unloved because her husband cannot stand to speak to her (or to anyone else for that matter) before he has been awake for two hours. If she takes personally his grunt in return to her cheerful greeting, she may feel hurt and unloved.

To be special and unique to each other does not mean that covenant-marriage partners are totally wrapped up in each other

Anytime we hear ourselves saying, "If you loved me, you would ...," we should recognize that we are expecting to be our partner's whole world. We need to deal with each other's expectations and the conflict that comes when we do not live up to them. But we must also recognize that expectations do not need to be tests of our partner's love and loyalty. Carlos and Amelia need to work on how they signal each other that they are distracted by other things, that they need a compliment for a well-prepared meal, and that they can take a moment or two to hug or share a few thoughts without being expected to spend the entire evening together. These are not questions of "Do you love me?" but of how they will work mutually to meet their needs and expectations.

F. Name one issue you have made a "test question" to judge your partner's commitment.

_____

Check at least one of the following ways you can move this issue out of the role of a relationship test. When this issue arises, I can—
❑ remind myself how much my mate loves me;
❑ react in a rational, rather than an emotional, way;
❑ think about how I am responding and decide not to make it a relationship test;
❑ count to 10;
❑ pray for patience and an extra measure of love for my spouse;
❑ discuss with my spouse why I feel unloved.

Problem 2: We retreat from the rest of the world. God made a covenant with Israel for it to become a nation of priests to serve the rest of the world (see Exodus 6:5), not just for God to have an exclusive, private relationship with the Israelites. Covenant marriage is also to be a base for joint ministry, not a retreat into seclusion with each other. The ministry of covenant marriage takes place both as a couple and as we support each other in our unique callings as individuals. Lessons 5 and 6 will focus on our ministry together as a couple. In this section we will focus on the role of covenant marriage in supporting the partners' individual callings.

Covenant partners are individuals, with individual callings as Christians. Jesus calls us individually, just as He did Andrew and Peter, James and Zacchaeus. A significant role for partners in covenant marriage, then, is supporting and encouraging each other in seeking to fulfill God's call as individuals.

G. Recall the two problems that develop when partners expect to be the whole world to each other.
   1. We take _____ every _____ and _____ of the partner.
   2. We _____ from the rest of the _____.

COVENANT PARTNERS ARE INDIVIDUALS
I alone will answer to God for the gifts and responsibilities God has given me. God is not going to look at me and say, "Oh, you are David's other half!" As I stand before the Lord each day of my life, I cannot turn to my spouse and

Expectations do not need to be tests of our partner's love and loyalty

place the blame for my failure to live God's purpose in my life. We are individually members of the body of Christ (see 1 Corinthians 12:27). As a member of that body, I am unique, different from all others, including my partner. Each of us has been given gifts, capabilities we are to use in our Lord's service (see 1 Corinthians 12:4-5).

H. **What is your GQ (gratefulness quotient) for your talents and abilities?**
   I can think of at least two talents I have. ❑ Yes ❑ No
   I often thank God for the abilities He has given me. ❑ Yes ❑ No
   I could complete this sentence easily: "I am special because. ..." ❑ Yes ❑ No
   I can name three significant contributions I make to my family. ❑ Yes ❑ No
   I share my giftedness in several ways at church. ❑ Yes ❑ No

If you answered at least three of the statements yes, you are well on your way to loving God, self, and others.

Jesus commanded us to love the Lord our God with all our heart, our soul, our mind, and our strength. Because we are each unique, however, *how* each of us is to show that love is not prescribed. We are to love God with our whole self—completely—and that means with all of the differences with which we were wonderfully made. As individuals we are to express our love for God in all aspects of living. Read Mark 12:29-30 and think about what it means for you personally to love God—

- with all your heart—with your emotions and feelings. How do you use your love, your excitement, your anger to build relationships with others and to make a difference in the world around you?
- with all your soul—with the very meaning and purpose of your life. How do your goals, the things that claim your primary attention, fit into your understanding of God's purposes?
- with all your mind—with the use of your intelligence and your thoughts. What TV shows, reading, study do you choose to fill your time? How do you use chances for learning, and how do you incorporate into your life what you have learned?
- with all your physical strength—with the use of your body. How do you abuse or nourish your physical self with nutrition, exercise, sexual expression, rest? Do you see your physical self as an integral part of your spiritual self and your relationship with God?

I. **As you read the questions above, perhaps you identified several areas for personal growth. List at least two ways you would like to change.**

   1. _____

   2. _____

   Are you willing to ask for your partner's help in accomplishing these changes? If so, how could your mate help you? Be specific.

   1. _____

   2. _____

We are to love God with our whole self—completely—and that means with all of the differences with which we were wonderfully made

To love God with all of our being was only half of Jesus' answer when He was asked about the most important commandment. He added to loving God that we are to love our neighbors as ourselves (see Mark 12:31). We are called as individuals to live our personhood in all of our relationships in life, with all of our neighbors, including "neighbor-spouse." And to do this, we must also love ourselves. We cannot give ourselves in sacrificial love to each other and to the world unless we first accept our worthiness as a gift. One significant covenant responsibility is for spouses to support each other's worth, to encourage each other to love self.

J. How have you affirmed your partner's worth during the past week? If you can't think of a specific instance, will you commit yourself to expressing affirmation to your spouse today? ❑ Yes ❑ No How?

_____

_____

Jesus' linking of two commandments to love God and love neighbor (including neighbor-spouse) has yet another significant application in covenant marriage. It is clear that Jesus intended these two commands to be flip sides of the same coin. We cannot love God without loving neighbor, and we cannot love neighbor without loving God. Even so, the two sides of love create a process of creative tension in marriage. Love for God emphasizes our individuality. Love for neighbor emphasizes our relationship with each other. From the balancing of these two aspects of marriage comes growth in a relationship.

TWO DIMENSIONS IN FOCUS
When we talk about loving God with all our heart, soul, mind, and strength, we are really talking about an individual's growth toward the life God intends for that person. The challenge of individuality, then, is the challenge to become all God intends for us to be as individuals.

Yet this cannot be the only goal of our lives. It has to be kept in balance with loving neighbor—including neighbor-spouse—as self. In other words, individual growth is to be balanced by giving attention to the other's needs and by nurturing our relationship with each other. Neither individual growth nor relational growth has greater value—each balances the other.

In marriage this dual focus results in two processes that appear to be in tension with each other yet together keep the relationship balanced and growing. These are uniqueness as individuals and unity as a couple.

Individuality
Just as two individual nations form an alliance for mutual support and benefit, covenant marriage is an alliance. Spouses maintain their uniqueness as individuals; each lives a life separate from the marriage, perhaps with specific friends or in a job, areas of interest, or church and community responsibilities that are not shared by the marital partner. Partners serve as encouragers and supporters as each uses and develops unique, individual gifts. We encourage each other to love self as a part of loving each other. As each other's ally, we cheer each other on. We may not always be involved in the same activities, but

Individual growth is to be balanced by giving attention to the other's needs and by nurturing our relationship with each other

47

we have a keen interest and involvement in what the other is doing.

Individuality brings the possibility of change to marriage. Individuality in marriage makes couples more flexible; during trying times the strength of both persons and their developed, unique gifts give couples more possibilities and experiences to draw from. Each of us can make a difference in our marriage. I can choose to act in surprising ways in marriage, not always reacting predictably to the imperfections and problems we face together.

Individuality requires trust. To allow both partners to follow their own callings and develop their own gifts requires mutual trust. We must feel that we can count on each other to be there when we need support and that the other is faithful to our covenant even when we are not together.

K. **What are some activities you prefer doing alone?**

_____

_____

How does your spouse feel about your time alone?

_____

_____

How can you share information about your individual activities that will help your spouse feel more included?

_____

_____

Unity adds depth to the relationship

Unity

Much like two nations merging into one and becoming an undivided people, the process of unity in marriage is a process of "you and I" becoming "we." The process of unity operates when partners work together to accomplish a task, make decisions together, and decide together what is important for their family. We share ideas, attitudes, and living space.

Unity builds intimacy. Unity adds depth to the relationship. It creates shared memories. We know what the other will say before it is said, because our common experiences help us understand each other. We are not alone; we face our troubles, sorrows, and joys together.

Unity requires the ability to resolve differences. When couples act as individuals, they can tolerate differences of opinion. But when they work together as a unit, those differences become critical. It is one thing to disagree about how to keep financial records or discipline children if we divide these jobs, each taking responsibility for one (individuality). But it becomes critical to reach an agreement if we try to work together on both jobs (unity).

L. **Rate yourself on your ability to work together with another person to accomplish a specific task. Circle the appropriate number.**

	Yes	Sometimes	Usually	Never
1. See others' point of view	1	2	3	4
2. Give them the benefit of the doubt	1	2	3	4
3. Disagree without being disagreeable	1	2	3	4
4. Able to forgive		2	3	4
5. Give and take, lead and be led	1	2	3	4
6. Renegotiate as the situation or persons change	1	2	3	4
7. Willing to say, "I was wrong"	1	2	3	4
8. Able to confront but not condemn	1	2	3	4

Total _____

If you scored below 16, you can probably work well with others.

To understand the relationship patterns created by individuality and unity, consider the task of wallpapering a room. If they operated individually, one partner would prepare the walls, taking down pictures and patching holes, while the other bought the paper. One partner would then entertain the children while the other hung the paper. They share the task; yet they divide it in such a way as to use or develop individual abilities. In the process they may not even be in the same room together much of the time.

If they approached the task in unity, on the other hand, the couple would shop for the paper together. They would then work together on each task of the job, one holding the tools for the other, one cutting and the other pasting, and so on. One might even smooth the top of the paper while the other smoothed the bottom. They would work together like two parts of a machine.

Which way is better? Neither. Many tasks can be approached from either way of relating. Both patterns are necessary for a healthy marriage. We sometimes operate as one unit and other times as individuals. Yet most marriages are a little more weighted toward one or the other. Some couples love each other deeply and enjoy telling each other about their thoughts and feelings. Yet most of their time and energy is spent separately. Other couples tend to do everything with each other. They may seem inseparable and perhaps even incapable of functioning without each other.

M. Check the responsibilities you and your partner work on individually. Write X beside those you work on together.
- ❏ Car care
- ❏ Paying bills
- ❏ Household tasks
- ❏ Child care
- ❏ Yard work
- ❏ Shopping
- ❏ Church work
- ❏ Civic duties

Where you place your emphasis in your marriage may indicate where your marital muscles are. The independence of couples who are strongly individualistic enables them to do many things well. These are divide-and-conquer people; she grows blue-ribbon gardens, and he fixes plumbing. On the other hand, unity couples find intimacy by sharing the most mundane of daily tasks; they grocery shop together and fold clothes together. They may use their joint tasks as built-in times for sharing thoughts and feelings.

We sometimes operate as one unit and other times as individuals

Strengths taken to the extreme may mean that a couple can function only one way. Strength can then become weakness. Couples who function only as individuals may begin to lead separate lives and feel like ships passing in the night. They may even find themselves thinking that they have little in common anymore, having grown apart.

Couples who focus only on unity may develop rigid patterns of living and working together that are difficult to change with changing needs and circumstances. If one is sick or away, the other cannot function. One cannot make needed decisions or take action without the other. Disagreement and conflict may be catastrophic, threatening the existence of the relationship.

N. State in your own words: What is the potential danger of couples functioning only as individuals?

_____

_____

What is the potential danger of couples functioning only as a unit?

_____

_____

Neither individuality nor unity is better than the other, just the balance of the other

No couple can keep these two processes in exact balance. At different stages of our marital life we may tend toward one or the other. For example, newlyweds are often highly united. Every task is done together; every conflict is major. Couples with growing children operate as allies more often than as a unit; there is no other way to cover the demands of a growing family than to divide the responsibilities and each shoulder some. Neither individuality nor unity is better than the other, just the balance of the other.

O. Place a dot on the following continuum representing your and your partner's primary pattern of relating when you were first married.

individuals   unit

Now write *X* on the continuum representing how you relate now.

Has your basic pattern of relating changed? ❑ Yes ❑ No If so, has the change been for the better or worse? ❑ Better ❑ Worse

One cold winter night two porcupines were trying to sleep together. They wanted to be as close as possible to share their warmth, but when they moved too close, they stuck each other with their quills. When they moved too far away, they became chilled. It took quite a long time of adjustment to find just the right position for the greatest amount of warmth and the least amount of pain.[1]

P. Think about a goal you and our partner have mutually agreed on. Write it here.

_____

What gifts do you have that will contribute to achieving this goal?

_____

What gifts does your spouse bring to this endeavor?

_____

What steps leading to the accomplishment of this goal can best be done—

individually? _____

together? _____

How can you affirm your mate's contribution throughout the process?

_____

> *The gifts each partner brings to the relationship must be nurtured so that both are able to fulfill their callings as unique servants of God in the world*

SUMMARY

Although marriage partners may initially have chosen each other for varied reasons, some of which have grown obsolete or failed to materialize, they must continually choose to be involved in a now-oriented covenant relationship. Covenant partners must avoid taking personally every action and word of the partner, so that issues become test questions of their love. Nor should they retreat from the rest of the world in choosing each other.

The marriage relationship should include patterns of relating that allow for individual effort and togetherness, depending on the task at hand.

Covenant partners seek to balance individuality and unity so that the responsibilities of family life are cared for appropriately.

The gifts each partner brings to the relationship must be nurtured so that both are able to fulfill their callings as unique servants of God in the world.

CHECKPOINT

The following review exercise is designed to reveal whether you have achieved the learning goals for lesson 3. Answer each question. Correct answers are given after the final question.

1. Which of the following statements best defines what it means to be a whole person in the marriage relationship?
   ❏ a. To love God with all of my being
   ❏ b. To love myself as an individual with worth and purpose
   ❏ c. To love self as a base for acting in love toward my neighbor-spouse
   ❏ d. All of the above

2. Which of the following does not express the wholeness of persons in the marriage relationship?
   ❑ a. Referring to the other as the better half
   ❑ b. Expecting to be the whole world to each other
   ❑ c. Seeking personal self-fulfillment and private spiritual growth
   ❑ d. All of the above

3. Which of the following formulas best allows for the nurturing of your gifts and those of your partner?
   ❑ a. Couples who function only as individuals
   ❑ b. Couples who function only as a unit
   ❑ c. Couples who keep individuality and unity in balance
   ❑ d. Couples who function neither as individuals nor as a unit

4. We can honor the uniqueness of our marriage partner by—
   ❑ a. taking personally every action and word of the partner;
   ❑ b. supporting the individual calling of each partner;
   ❑ c. choosing the partner on a daily basis as a special person;
   ❑ d. retreating into seclusion with each other.

5. List three of your mate's gifts in column 1. List three of your own gifts in column 2.

Mate's Gifts	My Gifts
_____	_____
_____	_____
_____	_____
_____	_____

Now check your answers.
1. d
2. d
3. c
4. b, c
5. Personal response

LOOKING AHEAD

How do two persons become one flesh? In the next lesson we will examine the biblical concept of oneness in marriage. What needs do you and your mate meet for each other? How do you complement each other? Your reciprocal relationship will be celebrated as one strength of a covenant marriage.

---

[1]Adapted from Joseph W. Maxwell, "A Rational-Emotive Approach to Strengthening Marriage," in Nick Stinnett, Barbara Chesser, and John DeFrain, eds., *Building Family Strengths: Blueprints for Action* (Lincoln: University of Nebraska Press, 1979).

Celebrating Our Unity

Lesson 4

LOOKING BACK

Is there any nicer feeling than to be affirmed by someone you love? In group session 3 you had the opportunity to hear words of praise from your mate about your special, unique place in his or her life. In turn, you affirmed your mate. Together you looked for opportunities to nurture your giftedness as individuals and as a couple in the days ahead.

Think about the ways you offered to help each other become more the person God called you to be. Living in a covenant relationship is an exciting, adventurous journey into new ways of thinking, feeling, sharing, and serving.

OVERVIEW

Lesson 4 calls for a celebration! You will be celebrating your oneness as a married couple. Have you recently thought about the miracle of the one-flesh principle in marriage? God's wonderful plan for two completely different individuals to merge their lives into one life together is certainly cause for rejoicing.

When we speak of *our* relationship, *our* home, *our* children, *our* memories, we are identifying some of the elements that link us together in marriage. What are some of the needs you and your spouse meet for each other? Ways you complement each other? Strengths that cement the bonding process? How can you build an even stronger union by applying the principles of covenant marriage?

When you complete this lesson, you will be able to—
• define what it means to be a couple;
• explain the biblical concept of oneness in marriage;
• identify needs that persons have met in the marriage relationship;
• assess the ways your mate and you complement each other in your marriage;
• affirm with your mate the strengths of your marriage relationship.

IN THE IMAGE OF GOD CREATED HE—US

"God created man in His own image, in the image of God created he him; male and female created he them" (Genesis 1:27). There is nothing more basic to being human than the relationship between man and woman. And together, male and female, we are the image of God. Three is a familiar ring here. In unit 1 we saw that marriage is used throughout the Bible as a picture—an

God's wonderful plan for two completely different individuals to merge their lives into one life together is cause for rejoicing

53

image—of God's covenant love. Now even in the act of creation we see man and woman providing a picture of who God is.

What is it about us that looks like God?

A. In which of the following ways are we like God?
- ❑ The way we look
- ❑ Knowledge of right and wrong
- ❑ Capacity for love
- ❑ Desire for justice
- ❑ Intelligence
- ❑ Power
- ❑ Creativity
- ❑ Feelings

Not Flesh and Blood but Authority and Responsibility

"Look, he has his daddy's mouth!" exclaims a happy grandmother over her new grandson. When we point out that children are the likeness of their parents, we are usually referring to flesh-and-blood resemblance—the color of hair and eyes, big hands, and long noses.

People are formed in the likeness of their parents in other ways. Sometimes we note that children are like their parents because of what they do: "She is just as happy-go-lucky and outgoing as her mother"; "he is going to be a farmer just like his dad."

In Genesis 1:26 God said, "Let us make man [humanity] in our image, after our likeness: and let them have dominion over the fish of the sea, and over the fowl of the air, and over the cattle, and over all the earth, and over every creeping thing that creepeth upon the earth." God did not say, "Let's give them two eyes like we have, and a heart, and make them warm-blooded mammals." This is what God says: "Let's make humanity like us and give them responsibility and authority over the world I have created."

We are a picture of God, then, in the way we have authority and use that authority responsibly in caring for creation. The world and our relationships with one another were not given to us as possessions to do with as we please. The owner—the creator God—has made us caretakers. As we look at the world around us with its polluted skies and water, threats of nuclear destruction, and slums and poverty, we may realize that humanity has not managed its responsibility well. Yet the primary focus for Christians is not only the sorry state of the world but also the witness we bear in it. We are to be in the world but not of the world (see John 17:14-18).

How can we be a witness in the way we use the authority and responsibility God gave us over the created world? We can begin by looking at the impact we are having in our daily lives on the physical environment. Many of the decisions we make about our lifestyle are couple decisions.

B. Rate the extent to which you and your mate have been involved in making the world a better place to live. 1 = not involved; 2 = somewhat involved; 3 = very involved.

Combating pollution	1	2	3
Conserving energy	1	2	3
Preserving natural resources	1	2	3
Saving endangered species	1	2	3
Responding to hunger relief	1	2	3
Church involvement	1	2	3
Volunteer mission service	1	2	3

We are a picture of God in the way we have authority and use that authority responsibly in caring for creation

What are some other ways we can use our responsibility and authority in a positive way? Janet and Robert Aldridge began a pilgrimage together into an unknown future based on their understanding of their responsibility as Christians for being an image of God in the world. As a couple, they were concerned about the threat of nuclear war destroying the world. Robert was earning a healthy income as an engineer developing nuclear weapons when together they decided this was not what they wanted their lives to stand for. He resigned and found other employment, and Janet also found employment as together they supported their children and their calling to be representatives of God in the world.[1] Their act did not end the nuclear threat; yet their lives represent the responsible role Christians are to have in caring for God's creation.

Not all of us are faced with a decision as dramatic as the decision the Aldridges made. Yet our daily lives are full of decisions that affect the world around us.

C. Have you as a couple taken a stand on a particular moral, social, or ethical issue? If so, why did you feel that you had a responsibility in this area?

_____

_____

We have responsibility not only for the world "out there" but also for the world inside the marital relationship. My spouse is part of God's creation. Do I treat my partner with respect, recognizing in this other person the wondrous work of God's creation? Or do I sometimes treat my partner like an object to be used for my own benefit?

Not Power but Love
One characteristic of God, then, is dominion—the responsibility and authority for creation. Yet the Bible is even more direct about another characteristic of God—God is love: "Beloved, let us love one another: for love is of God; and every one that loveth is born of God, and knoweth God. He that loveth not knoweth not God; for God is love" (1 John 4:7-8). God may exercise responsibility and authority, but the very essence of God is love. And the greatest commandment we are given as God's children is to love! We are to love both God and neighbor (see Matthew 22:36-40; Mark 12:28-34; Luke 10:27).

Another way we look like God, then, is in how we love one another. Love qualifies dominion. For example, you might hear, "She is outgoing like her mother; she always makes friends with lonely folks and helps them out" or "She is outgoing like her mother; she has parties all the time and really likes to put on a show." Just as there are many ways to be outgoing, there are also many ways to exercise dominion, to have responsibility. God is love and exercises dominion by wooing us and telling us the consequences of our sin, not by forcing us. God does not stand with hands on hips ordering us about. "God so loved the world, that He gave His only begotten Son, that whosoever believeth in Him should not perish, but have everlasting life" (John 3:16). Some power!

God wants to influence us, to convince us to change our ways. Jesus was clear about the changes God wants from us, the ways we are to live our lives. And then

Another way we look like God is in how we love one another

God gives us the freedom to choose for ourselves, although there is no doubt that the sacrificial love of Christ's life, death, and resurrection is a powerful influence.

The tactics we use to try to influence each other as marital partners are to reflect God's ways with us. Certainly, all of us want our partners to change some of their ways. If you thought 30 seconds, you could probably name at least three ways you would like for your partner to change. The change might be anything from picking up dirty socks to remembering to write check amounts in the checkbook.

How do you try to get your partner to change? Sometimes my behavior may indeed reflect God's ways; I tell my partner what I want, and I invite change. I may even suggest a contract to help us get change started, and I take the first step. Other times, however, the picture of God in my life is tarnished by my threats and attempts to force my partner to change: "If you don't do this, then I'm going to. ..." Instead of inviting my partner, I try to force change. Instead of respecting freedom, I try to box my partner in so that there are no other choices but to do it my way.

Responsibility and love are not individual characteristics; they are relational characteristics

D. Write *A* for *agree* or *D* for *disagree* in front of each of the following statements.

____ God gives us the freedom to change—or not to change.

____ I should give my mate the freedom to change—or not to change.

____ If my partner does not change, I have the right to try to force change.

____ One positive way to invite change is to suggest a contract and take the first step myself.

____ The change I want from my mate may not be in his, her, or our best interest.

____ I must respect my mate's decisions about his or her personal choices even if I do not like them.

Not Me but Us

When we talk about responsibility and love instead of noses and complexion, our understanding of God's image no longer rests in the individual. We can examine one person's nose and complexion. But we cannot examine one person's responsibility and love. Responsibility and love are not individual characteristics; they are relational characteristics. God was in relationship with the Son before the beginning of the world (see John 1:1-2). In Genesis 1 God created humanity male *and* female; it is the *and*, the relationship between us, that is the image of God. *I* cannot look like God; only *we* can.

For Christians, the original responsibility given man and woman to be caretakers of God's creation has been given in new language; we are to be on mission to the world. In addition, our love for each other is to serve as a picture for the world of Christ's sacrificial love for the church (see Ephesians 5:25). What kind of picture are we giving?

E. If you drew a picture of your marriage, which of these descriptions would it most resemble? Check one.
   ❑ A landscape full of growing things
   ❑ A seascape with high waves and wind
   ❑ A tranquil bay on a lush, green island

❏ A parched desert with little life
❏ A city street with honking horns and crowded sidewalks

ONE PLUS ONE = ONE

"A man leaves his father and his mother and cleaves to his wife, and they become one flesh" (Genesis 2:24, RSV). We are unique and wonderfully made as individuals; as we discussed in lesson 3, we do not give up our individuality when we marry. Yet the marriage is a flesh-and-blood reality. Marriage is not just two individuals linked together with a marriage license. The two partners' personality characteristics, goals, gifts, feelings, and quirks are like the different colors on an artist's palette. How they are blended, put in contrast with each other, and worked together to make something new, a painting one could not have imagined only by looking at the colors themselves—that is marriage. The paints are real; they have vibrance all their own, but so does the painting. Someone can point to the individual colors in the painting, but there is a difference—they have become a part of one another. In the same way, Paul says that in marriage not only are we to love each other as we love ourselves, but we are also each other's body (see Ephesians 5:28-29). We are part of each other.

Our Uniqueness as a Couple

We are part of each other because we develop a life together that is different from the life of every other couple. Just as we as individuals are unique, there is no other marriage like ours. We have woven together our needs, our strengths, our goals, our interests, and our histories to make a marriage painting unlike any other. We differ from other couples in many ways.

Just as we as individuals are unique, there is no other marriage like ours

F. One code we use to let the other know we are angry is to—

_____

One long-term, shared goal is to be able to—

_____

One story we enjoy telling our friends is about the time we—

_____

Our system for getting everyone off in the morning is for me to—

_____

while my partner—

_____

Birthdays around our house are usually celebrated by—

_____

One thing I usually do for the children (pet) is—

_____

while my partner takes care of—

_____

I let my partner know not to disturb me by—

_____

Our marriage is different from that of our close friends because we—

_____

We have shared dreams that direct our lives, even though we may never have actually discussed them

Ways we communicate our feelings. When Molly accidentally slammed a cabinet door, she yelled, "I didn't mean it." Normally when she slams doors, it is her way of saying: "I'm mad. Stay out of my way!" Every marriage develops codes, both words with special meanings and actions that speak clear messages. Some signals might never be noticed by someone other than the partner—the raised eyebrow that means "Can we get the kids to bed early?" or the crooked smile that means "I'm really upset."

Our dreams and goals. We have shared dreams that direct our lives, even though we may never have actually discussed them. The way we spend time and other resources is a clue to what those shared dreams are. Saving money has different meanings for different couples—to send children to school, to buy a home, to be prepared for retirement. Couples also have daily goals that direct what they do—jogging together to stay fit, keeping one evening free to visit with family.

Inside stories and jokes. Couples have shared stories and jokes that are a part of their life together. "Remember the time you lost your keys?" The story itself does not have to be told; both partners laugh at the memory. We have our own history together, shared moments of joy and sorrow, and stories that are better each time we remember them.

Specialized routines for daily life. Couples develop well-oiled patterns of living together that arise from their needs, gifts, and ways of doing things. Getting ready in the morning, doing chores, parenting children, and communicating sexual needs are just a few.

Special celebrations or rituals. Partners develop unique ways to mark special events or times in their relationship. Certain foods and activities remind us of past times and come to be part of the history we share.

Ways we divide home responsibilities. Every couple has unique patterns of carrying out the responsibilities of home and family, everything from who puts out the garbage to who writes letters and addresses Christmas cards.

Invisible boundaries. Every couple develops invisible boundaries in their home that mark off private territory. The top of a desk, a kitchen-cabinet top, certain rooms in the home are well known as belonging to one or the other or being a haven for common junk collecting. We also develop patterns of sharing space that change with our needs. For example, we know when not to disturb each other and when the other welcomes our presence.

Other ways we are unique. You and your spouse are different from other marital couples in many ways. Shared interests, political beliefs, and the church's role in your relationship are a few examples; you may think of others.

This Is Who We Are!
As we look together at who we are and how our marriage has developed in unique ways to fit our needs as individuals, we can celebrate how wonderfully we are made as a couple. Most of our ways as a couple developed without our being aware of what was happening. In other ways we may have made intentional efforts at developing a relationship uniquely suited to our needs.

G. Sometimes it is necessary to change a pattern of relating that is not working for you. Check the phrases that illustrate intentional changes you have made in the way you—
❏ settle a conflict;   ❏ handle stress;
❏ get over hurt feelings;   ❏ get exercise;
❏ deal with grief;   ❏ spend leisuretime.

As we look at the ways our relationship is unique, we may also identify areas in which change is needed. How clearly is God's image visible in our relationship with each other? Some ways we relate to each other may be based on power tactics instead of love and concern for each other's needs. Our relationship may in some ways interfere with instead of strengthen our Christian ministry.

H. How do you exert power in your relationship? Check any of the following ways you may have tried to exercise your power.
❏ The silent treatment   ❏ Pouting
❏ Holding on to the purse strings   ❏ Tears
❏ Physical domination   ❏ Temper tantrums
❏ Withholding affection

PATTERNS IN OUR RELATIONSHIP
Like the opposite pulls on a compass of the north and south poles, there are pulls in marriage relationships. We identified two of these in lesson 3, the pulls of individuality and unity. The warmest, sunniest marital climates are those in which these two pulls are roughly equal—like the tropical zones around the equator. Either one taken to the extreme leads to a less appealing climate. The cold at one pole is in the marital relationship; partners are so separate that little warmth exists between them. At the other pole the cold is for the individuals; they are so involved with each other that their individuality is frozen. Few people live on the equator and keep these pulls in balance. Some couples are more united, and some are more individualistic, but even though they major on one pole, the other pole still pulls somewhat in their relationship.

Another set of poles also pulls on couples—difference and similarity.

Opposites Attract
In every marriage we can identify ways we differ from each other. You might initially have been attracted to your partner because you sensed that here was someone who was strong where you were weak, who could complete you. You

As we look together at who we are and how our marriage has developed in unique ways to fit our needs as individuals, we can celebrate how wonderfully we are made as a couple

may not have even been aware of your differences until after marriage, when they became all too apparent!

Differences can be a source of comfort and security ("I can't add two numbers twice and get the same answer, but she does a great job of keeping our books"). Differences can also be a source of aggravation ("I don't know how she can live in this kind of clutter; I like to have things neat and tidy").

The ways couples are opposite to one another are many. Here are a few.

1. Time of day you are at your best—morning vs. evening
2. Living space—neat vs. messy
3. Relationships with others—shy vs. outgoing
4. Money—spender vs. saver
5. Basis for decisions—thoughts vs. feelings
6. Ways to do things—planned vs. spontaneous
7. Attitude toward life—playful vs. serious
8. Ways to spend free time—stay-at-home vs. adventuresome

I. Circle the statements above that represent ways you and your partner are alike. Underline the statements that illustrate ways you are different. Count the number of circles and lines. Are you more alike or different?

A couple is unlikely to be different in all of these dimensions. If they were, they might have had difficulty getting together in the first place! Yet you may identify several areas in which you and your partner are totally different. The differences between us are the paint on the palette; how do we as a couple put those differences together?

Differences make harmony and cooperation possible. Like singing different parts of the same song, partners' strengths in different areas complement each other. Some of our differences fit together like a hand in a glove, like the one who loves to cook and hates to clean and the other who hates to cook but loves to clean. We can appreciate our differences as ways that together we can be what we could not be alone.

J. Write one hand-in-glove way you and your spouse complement each other.

_____

Differences require compromise. On the other hand, some differences between us create conflict. Differences in how we think children ought to be disciplined or ways we want to spend money, for example, often have to be resolved in some way. Usually that means compromise.

Compromise means that we each move toward common ground and away from our original position. We move toward being more in agreement, being more alike. As a result, as individuals in relationship, we make changes that lead to greater balance. We strengthen our weak spots.

K. An old adage says, "If both of you see everything alike, one of you is unnecessary!" Write one difference between you and your spouse that you have found to be a strength in your relationship.

_____

The differences between us are the paint on the palette; how do we as a couple put those differences together?

Two Peas in a Pod

As you looked through a short list of differences in the previous section, you found some ways you and your partner are alike. There may be others, such as how you feel about political beliefs, the place of faith in your lives, how to rear children, and the role of church and family in your relationship.

Like our differences, similarities are both a strength and a challenge for our relationship.

Similarities are the basis for friendship and intimacy. I am not alone in the world (see Genesis 2:18); this other person feels as I do, thinks as I do on some of the issues in life that are important to me. We are kindred spirits.

Similarities require balance. Like difference, however, similarity is not just a source of comfort. Similarity can also be a source of difficulties. If we both are serious persons who have difficulty taking time away from the demands of life to refresh mind and spirit, our life together may become one-sided. We may be so concerned about thinking alike and feeling alike that we try to ignore little differences between us. In doing so, unfortunately, we may miss the gifts our individuality can bring to the marriage. For the very-serious-about-life couple, one partner may have an urge to take off one Saturday for a picnic but ignore the thought because it does not fit what "we" think we ought to accomplish.

L. If you suddenly did something that is out of character for you, how would your mate respond?
   ❏ Take you to the emergency room
   ❏ Roll with the punches
   ❏ Find it amusing
   ❏ Ignore it
   ❏ Act on it before you changed your mind

For us to find ways we can develop our differences is important. From those differences we can develop a more balanced and growing relationship.

M. Is there a hobby or sport you have put on the back burner because it is not an activity "we" would enjoy? Can you spend some time developing your interest in this activity without your mate feeling threatened? ❏ Yes ❏ No

Our Strength Is ...

Every couple has differences, and every couple has similarities. Most couples do not live with their similarities and differences in perfect balance. One or the other of these poles tends to pull more strongly in our relationship. You may be able to identify which is stronger by looking at the list on page 60 and discovering whether difference or similarity seems to hold more sway. There are two other ways we can identify our strongest pole.

The way we handle household responsibilities. Couples who are pulled more by difference tend to divide chores into lists for each partner. One does the mowing, the other the trimming; one does the laundry, the other the cooking. Couples who are pulled more by similarity tend to take turns; one mows this week, the other next week. Or a couple who has a more even balance of difference and similarity may divide some chores and take turns on others.

The way we handle conflict. Couples who are pulled more by difference

Most couples do not live with their similarities and differences in perfect balance

tend to offset each other when they experience conflict. One partner focuses on being rational and thoughtful, the other on feelings and emotions. One partner yells; the other cries. One partner insists on talking; the other refuses to say a word. Couples pulled more by similarity tend to address conflict in the same way—they try to out-reason, out-yell, or out-silent-treatment each other. Couples who have an even balance of difference and similarity may use both kinds of conflict management.

N. Place a dot on the following continuum to express the way you and your partner handle household responsibilities. Write *X* on the continuum to indicate how you handle conflict.

---

similarity   difference

CELEBRATING OUR STRENGTHS AND MAKING CHANGES

There is no one way of being married that is best. Not even a perfect balance of individuality and unity, similarity and difference is ideal. Every couple must look at their own needs and gifts, their own commitments and callings. These can help determine patterns of relating that best fit your unique relationship.

Sometimes when you are experiencing problems and see glaring needs for change in your marital relationship, it is difficult to see the strengths. But behind every problem is strength.

Susan and Matt argue about how much time to spend with aging parents. Susan wants to include them in vacations and holidays; Matt wants more time alone with Susan. Matt brings a gift to the marriage—a focus on nurturing the relationship with private time for renewal. Susan also brings a gift—a focus on their responsibility as a couple for broadening the circle of their love to include others, even their own family. Such a focus can lead to a sense of purpose in the marriage that also strengthens marital bonds. Behind Susan and Matt's arguments is strength if they learn to use it. They can learn to appreciate their differences through compromise. They can also see that they are alike; they share a common concern for the meaning and fulfillment of their covenant relationship.

O. Which difference between you and your mate causes the greatest problem for you?

What is one compromise ...

on your part ...

---

on his or her part ...

... that would help bring about a workable solution?

Sometimes when you are experiencing problems and see glaring needs for change in your marital relationship, it is difficult to see the strengths. But behind every problem is strength

As Matt and Susan work through their differences, their relationship will change. A marriage is always changing. The question is, Do we want some of the change we experience to be intentional? If we seem to agree on almost everything, perhaps we need to look for ways we can highlight and use our differences to strengthen our relationship. The one who has picnic urges on Saturday afternoons needs to be encouraged to pay attention and highlight these different thoughts. Or if we seem to stand on opposite sides of many issues, like Matt and Susan, we may need to learn to highlight our common ground. In the midst of our change, however, we need to keep sight of the fact that our marriage is unlike any other—and be thankful.

P. Select one or more of these actions you could take to express your gratitude for your mate during the coming week.

If You Are the Wife
❑ Spend time with him and his favorite hobby.
❑ Fix his favorite dinner.
❑ Give him a night out with the guys.
❑ Buy him a new "toy."
❑ Wear something he likes.
❑ Compliment him often.
❑ Do one of his chores for him.
❑ Pray daily for him.
❑ Spend time in Bible study with him.

If You Are the Husband
• Share her favorite activity with her.
• Take her out to dinner.
• Give her a night away from the kids.
• Buy her something personal.
• Send her flowers.
• Compliment her often.
• Fix something that needs repairing.
• Pray daily for her.
• Spend time in Bible study with her.

A marriage is always changing. The question is, Do we want some of the change we experience to be intentional?

SUMMARY

As male and female created in God's image, each couple is to exercise responsibility and respect in the way they treat the world outside and inside their marital relationship. When we love each other, we are most like God. The way we try to influence each other should reflect God's ways with us.

Responsibility and love are relational characteristics. Our marriages give us the opportunity to develop lives together that are different from the life of every other couple. We meet each other's needs and complement each other in a way that is unique from other married couples.

Two of the poles that pull on couples are difference and similarity. Both our differences and our similarities can be developed into strengths that result in a more balanced, growing relationship.

CHECKPOINT

The following review exercise is designed to reveal whether you have achieved the learning goals for lesson 4. Answer each question. Correct answers are given after the final question.

1. **Our uniqueness as a couple is shown in all but which one of the following ways?**
   ❑ a. How we communicate our feelings

    ❑ b. How we celebrate special occasions
    ❑ c. How we divide home responsibilities
    ❑ d. How we imitate others' marriages

2. Check two sets of poles that pull on couples.
    ❑ a. Difference and similarity
    ❑ b. Opposites and carbon copies
    ❑ c. Individuality and unity
    ❑ d. Intuition and reason

3. Fill in the blanks to explain how differences can be strengths in a marriage.
    a. Differences make _____ and _____ possible.
    b. Differences require _____.

4. Fill in the blanks to identify two strengths of similarity.
    a. Similarities are the basis for _____ and
    _____.
    b. Similarities require _____.

5. The strongest pole in my marriage relationship is (check one) ❑ difference ❑ similarity.

6. Write *T* for *true* and *F* for *false*.
    ___ a. A marriage is always changing.
    ___ b. The best way to deal with differences is through compromise.
    ___ c. When we agree on most things, we should discourage different thoughts.
    ___ d. One way to highlight our common ground is to avoid conflict.

Now check your answers.
1. d
2. a, c
3. a. harmony, cooperation; b. compromise
4. a. friendship, intimacy; b. balance
5. Personal response
6. a. *T,* b. *T,* c. *F,* d. *F*

LOOKING AHEAD

Have you ever looked at another couple and wondered why they married each other? Perhaps they appeared physically mismatched or their personalities were direct opposites. Other couples may seem like the perfect couple.

In lesson 5, "Called to Purpose," you will be reminded of the reasons for entering a marriage. How can your marriage be more purposeful? How can the biblical basis for marriage give your marriage more meaning?

---

[1]Jim Wallis, *Peacemakers: Christian Voices from the New Abolitionist Movement* (San Francisco: Harper & Row, 1983), 7–13.

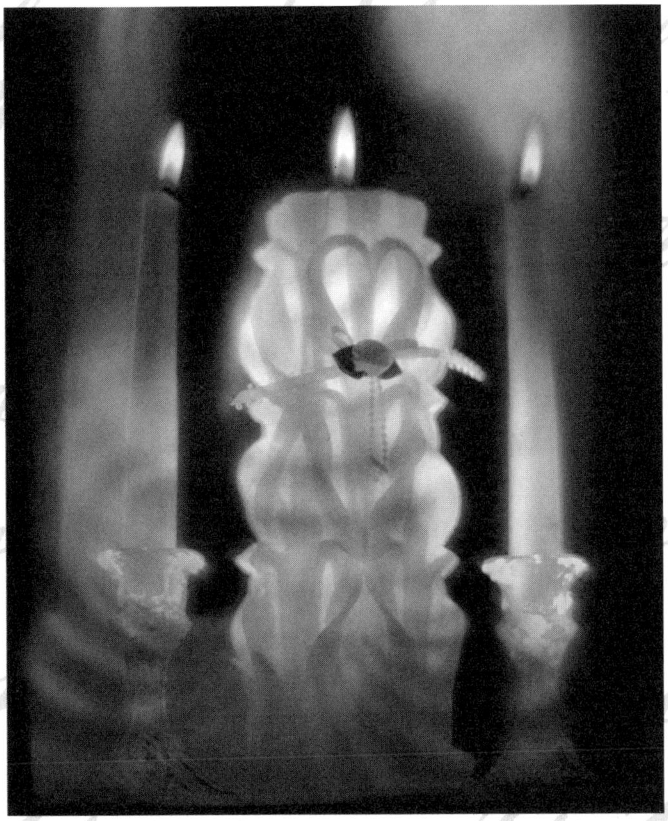

Unit 3

A Journey Outward

CALLED TO PURPOSE

Lesson 5

As covenant partners relate to each other in love and care, they show God's love

LOOKING BACK

In unit 2, "A Journey Inward," you were asked to assess your gifts as an individual and as a couple to celebrate the uniqueness of your relationship. Do you recall some of the special talents and abilities you identified in yourself? your partner? How are you encouraging the development of these gifts on a regular basis?

What unique features of your marriage did you discover? What ways of relating work for your marriage that encourage each partner to become the person God intended?

How are you attempting to balance the poles of individuality and togetherness, difference and similarity? As you think about these questions, perhaps you will want to review some of the material covered previously.

OVERVIEW

Think about a journey that took you beyond the familiar surroundings of home to a completely new location. How did you feel about the trip? Was it exciting? threatening? Did you long for home or want to stay there forever?

Any journey outward has an element of risk. We don't know what's out there. But who would want to miss the beauties of our world in order to stay in a safe, secure environment? In unit 3 we will begin an outward journey, beyond the confines of our marriage relationship. How does your marriage influence the world around you? How do you and your mate function in the worlds of home, church, and community?

In lesson 5 you will begin to discover the purposes for which God brought you together. When you complete this lesson, you will be able to—

- identify and give priority to the reasons you and your mate entered a marriage relationship;
- list reasons for entering a marriage relationship;
- determine how you can strengthen your purposes in marriage.

CALLED TO BE AND CALLED TO DO

As covenant partners relate to each other in love and care, they show God's love. The intimacy that develops between husband and wife portrays the personal, intimate love that Jesus taught us is Godlike. In the Letter to the Ephesians Paul told spouses that they are to love each other as their own bodies,

66

nourishing and cherishing each other (see Ephesians 5:28). Our calling as Christians in marriage, then, includes being loving and intimate with each other. To live in a covenant marriage means that we are called to be intimate and loving with each other as a sign of who God is.

A. Which of these best describe(s) intimacy as it applies to your marriage?
❑ **Freedom of sexual expression**
❑ **Being together a lot**
❑ **Feeling close to each other**
❑ **Able to talk about everything**

However, covenant marriage involves more than just being loving and intimate with each other. God also expects us to answer the call to servanthood. As covenant partners, we are to do God's will. Both God's covenant with Israel and the covenant with the church through Jesus Christ have had purposes beyond intimate fellowship between the people and God. Israel was to be a light among the nations of the world to bring all people into fellowship with God. The church, too, has a purpose beyond serving itself. Paul wrote that marriage is to be modeled after Christ's relationship with the church (see Ephesians 5:32). Covenant marriage, then, has a purpose beyond intimate fellowship between partners.

Priscilla and Aquila were a New Testament couple who took seriously their calling as covenant partners. Paul called them his "fellow workers" (Romans 16:3, RSV). Together they worked in their business of tent making (see Acts 18:3), instructed others in the faith (see Acts 18:26), and welcomed Paul and no doubt others into their home (see Acts 18:3). We have no record of what their private life with each other was like, but it is clear that their relationship with each other was the basis for an effective shared ministry beyond taking care of each other.

B. Can you think of a modern Priscilla and Aquila in your church or community? Describe how they model a team approach to ministry.

_____

_____

Covenant marriage includes both being intimate and loving with each other and doing God's will as partners called into service together. We need to care for each other, to nourish each other. But we also need a sense of direction and purpose in our life together beyond mutually meeting needs.

Without intimacy and love there is no relationship to begin with. Our covenant together requires steadfast love that needs to be nourished (see Ephesians 5:29) by our intimacy. We are intimate when we let each other know what we think, how we feel, and what is important to us. Sometimes we do not have to speak to be intimate; a look, a gesture, a touch can communicate. Often, though, intimacy is deepened when we can put words to what we experience. Looks and gestures usually assume that we already understand each other. Words help our partner understand us in new ways.

We need a sense of direction and purpose in our life together beyond mutually meeting needs

C. Try this approach to expressing intimate thoughts during the coming week. Ask your spouse to listen to what you say, then to repeat it to you as exactly as possible without comment. This technique will help you know how well you are communicating your thoughts. If you did not get the feedback you wanted on the first try, say it again until your spouse can verbalize your feelings to your satisfaction. Then offer to do the same for your spouse.

We are most intimate with each other when we share not only our thoughts and feelings but also our thoughts and feelings about each other. To tell you how I feel about my work is intimate sharing, but to tell you how I feel about you is even more intimate. Even though a risk is taken, when we share positive thoughts and feelings with each other, we strengthen the bonds between us. When we share anger and frustration with each other, we have opened the way for bridging the barriers between us, even though other barriers may possibly be built.

D. Rank the degree to which you communicate your thoughts and feelings with your spouse in each of the following areas. Place a check in the appropriate column for each area.

	Seldom	Occasionally	Never
1. Things that please me			
2. Things that displease me			
3. Sexual needs/pleasures			
4. Finances			
5. When I need help			
6. When I am upset			
7. When I am sad			
8. When things aren't going well at work or home			
9. Family problems			
10. Hopes and dreams			

As important as intimate communication is, however, most of married life is centered in the chores and tasks we face together. Intimate relating is intense and demanding. It is important, but partners cannot spend all of their time focused on telling each other how they feel and think about each other and their marriage. Our tasks, our callings to work as covenant partners in God's kingdom demand our attention, too. There must be both being and doing.

PURPOSE IN OUR MARRIAGE
When couples decide to marry, they rarely do much organized thinking about the purposes of their marriage. For many, intimacy is the critical factor; they cannot bear to live without each other. For others, shared values and dreams promise a life of shared purpose. There are many other reasons for getting married and staying married. The reasons we married in the first place often fade, and other reasons for staying married develop. As you study your own covenant marriage, it may help to identify why you made the decision to marry and why you decide each day to stay married.

When couples decide to marry, they rarely do much organized thinking about the purposes of their marriage

Providing Protection

Many spouses marry not only because they want to move into a lifetime commitment with each other but also because they are running away from something else. Some people get married to escape an unhappy relationship with parents. It seems that they can become adults and separate from the families they grew up in only by starting families of their own. Other spouses choose each other because they are afraid of being alone. Perhaps they have never been alone, or perhaps they are afraid that if they do not snatch the opportunity, they may spend the rest of their lives alone.

Sometimes spouses choose partners because they seem to offer protection from something the spouses fear in themselves. Susan married Mark in part because he was strong and seemed always sure of himself; he could protect her from her uncertainty. Mark married Susan because she was so quiet and never seemed to get angry. She offered him protection from a marriage like his parents', in which there had been loud, hurtful conflict that finally ended in divorce.

If we admit it to ourselves, many of us are looking for security when we marry; either marriage itself or our partner's characteristics look from our perspective like a safe harbor from a frightening expanse of life's ocean.

Even though this protection does not seem like a firm foundation for beginning a marriage relationship, it is clear that our reasons for staying married may not be the same as the reasons for getting married in the first place. Susan may learn that Mark is too sure of himself, even when he ought to be uncertain, and that she has to take equal responsibility for what happens in their life together. Mark may learn that Susan may not express her anger loudly, but she gets angry nevertheless, and he has to reckon with her feelings. Even though we learn that we may not be able to protect each other from our fears, we can face them together.

Protection is one reason people get married. But if it is the only reason a couple stays married, the marriage may seem stale and empty. Spouses who stay married for purposes of protection are like two persons taking shelter from a storm in the same barn. Unless they begin a relationship with each other, share themselves with each other, and join their efforts and interests, they will remain two individuals rambling around an empty barn.

Many of us are looking for security when we marry

E. Check the fears you hoped to avoid by marrying your mate.
- ❑ Fear of financial insecurity
- ❑ Fear of being alone
- ❑ Fear of not having children
- ❑ Fear of social rejection or teasing
- ❑ Fear of angry confrontations
- ❑ Fear of caring for all of your own needs
- ❑ Fear of the possibility of divorce
- ❑ Fear of something you see in yourself

Have you felt protected from the fears you checked? ❑ Yes ❑ No

Coping with Social Pressure

Relationships with other people, like parents and friends, may press some couples to marry. Pregnancy, for example, is the reason many couples marry: other people push them to marry either by what they say or by their speculation about what will be said and thought if they do not marry. Others may also push one or both partners to marry because the relationship seems right to them; perhaps a parent fears that if the child does not marry this person, he or she may not have another chance. Parents may want to feel that their child has settled down, or they may want grandchildren.

Some couples also stay married because of social pressure. The only thing that holds them together is the fear of what others might say and do if they divorced. Like protection, coping with social pressure is not a strong enough purpose for a covenant marriage. Marriages that begin or continue because of social pressure may well become effective, loving covenant relationships but only if the partners develop intimacy and effective direction for their relationship.

Providing Status

Some people marry because of the status it offers. Perhaps the flash of a diamond ring, being the first in the group of friends to get married, or the stability or belonging the partner's family offers that has been missed in a person's own family life pushes that person toward marriage. Marrying to gain status is much like marrying to cope with social pressure. The difference is that the push comes more from within the person than from others.

Like coping with social pressure, some choose to stay married because of the status it offers them. They do not want to be known as a divorced person or to give up the identity that comes from being married to their partner.

F. **Rate the degree to which you were influenced by your family, friends, church, and social expectations about your marriage partner by checking the appropriate column beside each statement.**

	A Lot	Some	A Little
1. What my friends thought about the person I dated was important to me.			
2. I would never have married someone my parents disapproved of.			
3. I would not have wanted to be single all my life.			
4. My choice of a mate was influenced by my church's teachings.			
5. A part of staying married has to do with how other people would feel about a separation or divorce.			

Meeting Economic Needs

Some couples marry to be taken care of economically. Of course, this is not as common as in the past since most women work and can be financially independent, and labor-saving devices in the home make it possible for both men and women to survive without a traditional homemaker to care for the home and meals. Still, it is cheaper for two to live together than separately; and this is at least a part of some couples' decisions to marry.

It is more common, however, for economic needs to figure into a partner's decision to stay married. The expense of two households, particularly if there are children to support, may be a factor that keeps a couple together.

Some people marry because of the status it offers

For many couples, economic needs are an important force in their marriage, because what gives their marriage real purpose and direction is spending money. Beth and Roy are such a couple. They spend their time together shopping, eating out, and seeing movies. Married for three years, they both work outside the home. The primary focus of their life together at the present is furnishing the home they just purchased. They spend hours together looking at furniture and carefully planning their purchases. One dream they enjoy talking about is taking a big vacation.

Even though taking care of economic needs and spending money are part of American life, economic security or spending money on ourselves cannot be the sole or central purpose of covenant marriage. There is nothing wrong with furnishing a home or traveling. But if this is our whole life together, our marriage becomes self-centered and deaf to the calling to minister to others.

G. Does our family budget permit us to—
   give to charitable and religious causes? ❑ Yes ❑ No
   tithe to our church? ❑ Yes ❑ No
   help care for our parents (or other extended family)? ❑ Yes ❑ No
   provide for emergencies? ❑ Yes ❑ No
   reflect concern for others outside our family circle? ❑ Yes ❑ No

Developing Intimacy

Most people respond to the question "Why did you get married?" by saying, "Because we loved each other." By *love* they mean that they had developed a level of intimacy that tied them together with the gentle bonds of understanding, sharing, and attraction. They did not want to face life without each other; instead, they wanted to share their lives as one. Intimacy between marital partners includes both sexual fulfillment and friendship.

Sexual fulfillment. Few marriages would be launched if it were not for the partners' sexual attraction to each other. Paul's teaching about marriage makes it clear that this is a valid reason for marrying (see 1 Corinthians 7:9,36).

Paul has often been misunderstood to be against sex because of the way 2 Corinthians 7:1 is translated: "Now concerning the matters about which you wrote. It is well for a man not to touch a woman" (RSV). But Paul was not antisex. He was probably quoting what someone among the Corinthians had been saying. Paul was introducing his subject: "Now I want to talk to you about what some have been saying, that it is more spiritual not to have sexual relations."

In verses 2-5 Paul went on to tell the Corinthians that their belief that they should avoid sex is wrong; they should not refuse each other in sexual relations. Marriage is to be a fully sexual relationship. Sex was intended by God to be a part of the marriage experience. Sex is part of God's good creation (see 1 Timothy 4:1-3).

Sexual intimacy is not only a reason Christians marry but also one of the reasons they continue to choose each other. The sexual relationship in covenant marriage builds the partners' intimacy with and commitment to each other: "This is the will of God ... that each one of you know how to take a wife for himself in holiness and honor, not in the passion of lust like heathen who do not know God" (1 Thessalonians 4:3-5, RSV).

The sexual relationship between covenant partners should build up each part-

Intimacy between marital partners includes both sexual fulfillment and friendship

71

ner as a person worthy of respect and honor. Partners are not to lust, which means to turn the other into an object to be used instead of a person to be loved.

Although the 1 Thessalonians passage addresses men, Paul makes it clear in 1 Corinthians that both husbands and wives have sexual needs and responsibility for the sexual relationship: "The husband should give to his wife her conjugal rights, and likewise the wife to her husband. For the wife does not rule over her own body, but the husband does; likewise the husband does not rule over his own body, but the wife does" (1 Corinthians 7:3-4, RSV).

One ongoing purpose of covenant marriage, then, is to fulfill the husband's and wife's sexual needs. Both husband and wife are responsible for the sexual relationship between them—it cannot be the responsibility of either alone.

The sexual relationship between partners is to be active, even though partners may have reasons to abstain at times from sexual relations. Paul spoke of agreeing to abstain from sex during a time of prayer (see 1 Corinthians 7:5), perhaps during times of crisis and when facing difficult decisions. Partners may also choose to abstain during times they are troubled, such as during grief over the loss of a loved one. But abstinence is to last only "for a season," and the sexual relationship needs to be restored to a significant role in the marriage.

Talking together, sharing experiences, building memories, and facing the future together create intimacy with each other

H. What role did sexual attraction play in your initial choice of your mate?
❑ A lot ❑ Some ❑ A little

What roles does sexual attraction play in your current relationship? Check all that apply.
❑ Sexual attraction is the chief factor in our staying together.
❑ Sexual attraction is significant but not the most important aspect of our marriage.
❑ Sexual attraction is one of the less satisfying aspects of our marriage.
❑ Sex with my spouse is often a very tender experience.
❑ My spouse and I have sex about as often as I want.
❑ Usually, my spouse and I are openly affectionate with each other.
❑ Sex with my mate is sometimes a very fun experience.
❑ My relationship with my mate is the closest I've ever had.

Friendship. Intimacy also includes being each other's friend. Partners share thoughts, feelings, dreams, and fears with each other. Talking together, sharing experiences, building memories, and facing the future together create intimacy with each other. The friendship that grows over the years between marital partners is one of the most important reasons spouses continue to choose each other, even as they learn all too well each other's faults and limitations as well as their gifts and strengths.

Spouses are friends with each other in many ways. We are friends when we share our hurts or embarrassments with each other that we would never dream of confiding in someone else. We are friends when we brag on something we are proud of or share a secret hope that we would never admit to any other. We are friends when we relax together; laugh at ourselves and each other; and, in so doing, find joy in being together, deepening our affection for each other. Finally, we are friends when we listen to each other talk over the things that interest us, worry us, or anger us, finding listening and concern in each other when others would be bored.

I. Test your friendship quotient with your mate by checking the appropriate column for each statement.

	Agree	Agree Somewhat	Disagree
1. My relationship with one of my friends is in some ways closer than my relationship with my spouse.			
2. My personality and that of my spouse seem to fit together well.			
3. My mate and I can talk about our deepest feelings and private thoughts.			
4. If I could choose one person to spend a day with, it would be my spouse.			
5. There is an excitement in my mate's and my relationship.			
6. My relationship with one of my children is in some ways closer than my relationship with my spouse.			

Accomplishing Common, Shared Goals

Finally, people marry because they share a purpose or a goal they can reach more fully together. The most common example is the birthing and rearing of children. A man and a woman may find that they share a common goal of being foreign missionaries, starting a summer camp for inner-city children, reclaiming abused land and turning it into productive farmland, or a myriad of other dreams big or not so big. They share a vision that in some way their marriage can make a difference in the world.

J. Complete the following sentences.

When we married, our dream was to—

_____

_____

The dream changed over time to become—

_____

_____

That dream was accomplished/is being accomplished by—

_____

_____

People marry because they share a purpose or a goal they can reach more fully together

73

Our latest dream is to—

_____

_____

IDENTIFYING OUR PURPOSES

Engaged couples do not often spend much time considering together their purposes for marrying. And before we are too critical of engaged couples, we must recognize that most of us as married couples do not often talk about our purposes in remaining committed to each other. Yet focusing on our purposes for being together can help us steer a more direct path toward meeting each other's needs and working toward God's purposes for our marriage. Here are some suggestions for identifying the purposes that influence your relationship.

Talk together about what was important to you in the beginning of your relationship and what is important now. Although we can assume that intimacy and common goals are likely to be a part of every marriage, as well as some of the other purposes discussed previously, these take a different shape in every marriage. Just as each spouse is a unique individual, every marriage is unique, with its own purposes and calling. No one can tell you what the purpose of your relationship is; it is between you and your partner and God. Other people may help point out your gifts and provide a different perspective on the decisions you make, but you and your partner alone, with the guidance of the Holy Spirit, can put the pieces together into a picture of what your marriage can and ought to be.

K. Which of these descriptions best pictures your marriage relationship?
- ❑ A sports car with a turbo engine
- ❑ A tugboat with a full load
- ❑ A hang glider peacefully floating above the clouds
- ❑ A jet circling the airport
- ❑ A vintage Volkswagen

Look for the threads of meaning in your common life. You may not have talked before about the purposes of your relationship, but your marriage has had direction nevertheless. Whether or not you discussed it, you and your partner have been working toward goals. You can identify these by looking at what is important to you. How do you spend your time together? What do you talk about together that makes you feel like a team, like partners? When, even for a fleeting moment, you have considered what life would be like if you were not married to your partner, what pulled you back into a sense of commitment? How is the world—your family, your neighborhood, your church, your community—different because you and your partner are married to each other? What do you enjoy doing together?

L. Take time to mentally answer each question in the preceding paragraph. Be prepared to share your answers with your partner at the next group session.

As you think about these questions, you may find threads of meaning that are the underlying strength of your relationship. You may also find yourself

Whether or not you discussed it, you and your partner have been working toward goals

wondering if your relationship can be more centered on what is important to both of you than it has been.

Expect purposes to change with time. Do not be surprised if the purposes that directed your relationship in the beginning no longer hold sway today. Just as the children who are the center of their parents' lives when they are infants grow up and leave home, many purposes of our life together change as our world changes. Often these changes are crises in our life together. We float directionless for a while, searching anew for the purpose God has for our lives. Even as we work on the major focus of our joint life, such as rearing children, we are confronted daily with the smaller tugs on us that together give our life meaning and purpose. These include relationships with neighbors, running a household, and involvement in our church and community.

M. **Identify the major focus of your life together as a couple. Use the following list as a guide or write your own.**
   - Getting out of school
   - Starting a business
   - Starting a family
   - Rearing children
   - Getting the kids through college
   - Mid-life crisis
   - Changing vocations
   - Caring for aging parents
   - Health problems

Look for the fruit of your joint efforts. As we look at our past and present together, we can try to imagine our corner of the world as it might be if we had never married. What difference has our relationship made? From the trees we have planted to the persons we have influenced with our love and care for each other and for them, what difference have we made?

N. **We are accustomed to bragging about our children or homes. What about our marriages? Describe some of your proudest moments as a couple.**

_____

_____

_____

_____

_____

What difference has our relationship made?

STRENGTHENING OUR PURPOSES

As we looked together at our relationship from the perspective of the guidelines above, we may have found threads of meaning and purpose we want to strengthen and work toward. We may also have found fruits of our relationship that are not what we would choose. Our marriage has made a difference both in our own lives and in the lives of others. Our marriage has had purpose and direction, even if not the purpose and direction we wanted.

Covenant marriage is centered in God's purposes and will. As we look at our life together, with God's help and guidance we can choose our directions for today and tomorrow.

O. Analyze the purpose and direction of your marriage today.

I feel that my partner and I are moving in the same direction. ❑ Yes ❑ No

We have more than one shared purpose in our life at this time. ❑ Yes ❑ No

We pause at appropriate intervals to evaluate our progress toward mutual goals. ❑ Yes ❑ No

Our goals as individuals are not in conflict with our goals as a couple and a family. ❑ Yes ❑ No

We are able to celebrate together the achievement of shared dreams and goals. ❑ Yes ❑ No

P. If you answered no to two or more statements above, write what you feel needs to happen in order for you and your mate to experience more purpose and direction in your relationship.

_____

_____

Focusing on our purposes for being together can help us meet each other's needs and work toward God's will for our marriage

SUMMARY

Covenant marriage involves more than being loving and intimate with each other. Covenant marriage involves answering the call to servanthood as covenant partners. The biblical examples of Priscilla and Aquila remind us that a loving relationship is the basis for an effective shared ministry.

There are many reasons to get married and stay married. Focusing on our purposes for being together can help us meet each other's needs and work toward God's will for our marriage.

CHECKPOINT

The following review exercise is designed to reveal whether you have achieved the learning goals for lesson 5. Answer each question. Correct answers are given after the final question.

1. Write *T* for *true* and *F* for *false*.

___ a. Covenant marriage requires a total focus on meeting the needs of your marriage partner.

___ b. An intimate relationship with our partner enhances our ability to be involved in God's work in the world.

___ c. When we share anger and frustration, we destroy the bridges to intimacy.

___ d. Friendship is one evidence of intimacy in marriage.

2. Which of the following is not one of the reasons people marry?

❑ a. Protection

❑ b. Social pressure

❑ c. Economic security

❑ d. Freedom from responsibilities

3. Fill in the blanks below to complete the list of guidelines for identifying the purposes that influence your relationship.

a. Talk together about what was _____ to you in the _____ of your relationship and what is

_____ now.

b. Look for the _____ of _____ in your common life.

c. Expect _____ to change with _____.

d. Look for the _____ of your joint _____.

4. Check daily mutual tasks that give meaning and purpose to your married life.

❏ Caring for children

❏ Planning a vacation

❏ Building/repairing something

❏ Sharing hopes and dreams

❏ Being involved in church

❏ Working in the yard

❏ Spending time with grandchildren

❏ Developing friendships

Now check your answers.

1. a. *F,* b. *T,* c. *F,* d. *T*

2. d

3. a. important, beginning, important; b. threads, meaning; c. purposes, time; d. fruit, efforts

4. Personal response

LOOKING AHEAD

To whom do you look when you need to cry, "Help"? Probably your mate. He or she is the source of help when errands need to be run, children picked up, planes met at the airport, or plumbers called.

Think about the ways you and your mate function as partners. In lesson 6 you will assess your partnership in the areas of what you do with each other, with others, and for others. Think about one action you could take to express your partnership in marriage.

Called to Partnership

Lesson 6

Unfortunately, we often think that the unwavering attention to each other in early marriage is how we should relate to each other all our married life

Looking Back

In lesson 5 we examined the purposes behind a couple's choice of each other as marriage partners. The purposes we examined fall into three categories: (1) What being married can offer the individuals (protection, coping with social pressures, providing status, economic security); (2) what the relationship with each other can offer each (sexual intimacy, friendship); and (3) what we can offer to others (children, family, church, community, world).

We looked at the purposes in the past and present that have directed our marital relationships—what was and is.

Overview

In lesson 6 we will direct our attention to what we want to be—the future of our marriage. We will consider the purposes beyond meeting our needs that give direction and meaning to our lives with each other. When we address this aspect of covenant marriage, which we call partnership, we stand shoulder to shoulder, facing a common work and calling together.

When you complete this lesson, you will be able to—
- define *partnership* as it is seen in marriage;
- list arenas in which your marriage operates as a partnership;
- assess your marriage as a partnership in—
  —what you do with your mate;
  —what you do, as individuals, with others;
  —what you do for others;
- take one action that will express your partnership in marriage.

Marriage—A Partnership

Of the three kinds of purposes that are the foundation for the decision to get married and stay married, partnership is listed last. Marriage usually begins because of what being married and the relationship with this special individual can offer. Early in the covenant relationship the partners are totally involved in their deepening commitment and intimacy with each other.

Unfortunately, we often think that the unwavering attention to each other in early marriage is how we should relate to each other all our married life. But to keep the center of attention of our marriage only on each other, on meeting each other's needs, is like children who grow into adults but refuse to recognize that they are not the center of the universe. Two-year-olds need to think of themselves as the center of everything; they are learning who they are as individuals with worth who are separate from the other individuals around them. But 20-year-olds who still see themselves as the center of everything are no longer doing what they need to do; instead, they need to find their place in God's scheme of things.

A. Rate your emotional maturity by checking the appropriate column for each statement.

	I respond more like a	
When I—	child	adult
1. hurt myself,		
2. don't get my way,		
3. am disappointed,		
4. get angry,		
5. have to wait,		
6. am criticized,		
7. am ignored,		

Now consider how your mate would rate you in each area.

Finding purpose and meaning for our marriage beyond taking care of each other's needs helps marriages grow up. As we lose ourselves together in service to the needs of the world around us, we find ourselves anew. If we genuinely share a common commitment, we find our partnership becoming more intimate, our marriage strengthened.

Some of the purposes that shape our lives just seem to happen. We did not choose our purposes; they seemed to choose us. We happen into shared responsibilities and commitments. Marsha, for example, was asked to teach a girls' missions-education group in her church's mission. She took the responsibility because she liked working with teenagers. Soon, however, not only were more girls coming than ever before, but she also became aware of the need for them to have a concerned, caring adult in their lives in addition to their parents. Gatherings outside the meetings were well attended, and the girls wanted to bring their boyfriends. Marsha asked her husband, Jim, to help her with the group. A year later Jim and Marsha were the leaders of an ever-growing youth group that saw significant changes in the lives of the young people involved. Marsha and Jim did not set out in the beginning to develop a youth ministry in an inner-city neighborhood. Yet now they recognize God working in their lives, bringing them together to a place of service. The experience has also deepened and enriched their commitment to and appreciation of each other.

B. Briefly describe one shared purpose you and your mate adopted that was not intentional but that evolved over time.

_____

_____

If we genuinely share a common commitment, we find our partnership becoming more intimate, our marriage strengthened

In lesson 5 you identified goals and purposes in your relationship that developed the same way Marsha and Jim's shared ministry developed. Before this study you may not have spent much time reflecting together about the partnership dimension of your marriage. Shared goals and purposes can also be the result of a shared search. We can pray together, search our gifts and our individual commitments, and intentionally build our partnership. We can commit ourselves together to search for God's will in our daily living.

C. Briefly describe one shared purpose you and your partner intentionally undertook.

_____

_____

Children benefit from growing up in a home with two parents who love them and love each other

No simple definition of God's purpose for every marriage can be given, because each couple is different. Some, like Marsha and Jim, find a calling that, at least for a period of time in the relationship, seems to be all-important. But purpose also involves daily decisions in the way partners choose to spend their money, use their time, and relate to others who touch their lives. These daily decisions in our shared life are just as important as the bigger decisions of career choices and whether to have children.

As we turn to some of the purposes that give focus to partnership, then, remember that not all of them need to apply to every marriage. But perhaps talking together about these arenas for partnership will help you assess the purposes of your marriage and determine how you want to strengthen or even change the direction your marriage is taking.

ARENAS FOR PARTNERSHIP

Spouses commonly find purpose and meaning in their relationship with each other in five arenas: parenting, careers, homemaking, church and community, and the world. You may think of other ways your marriage is a partnership as you consider these five general arenas.

Parenting

If we conducted a survey about the purpose of marriage beyond taking care of spouses' needs, we would most likely find "having children" at the top of the list. Despite the large numbers of single parents, our society still considers the marriage of a child's parents part of an ideal environment for a growing child. Children benefit from growing up in a home with two parents who love them and love each other.

D. Check the type of family unit you grew up in.
   ❑ Two parents + one child
   ❑ Two parents + children
   ❑ One parent + one child
   ❑ One parent + children
   ❑ Grandparents + child(ren)
   ❑ Other: _____

How has your family of origin influenced your decision about having children?

_____

_____

Children can also provide their parents a sense of responsibility and commitment as they work together in behalf of their children. There is nothing like birthing and bringing home a baby who depends totally on them to bring a couple to a keen sense of shared responsibility. The myths about having a baby to pull a marriage together have at least some basis of truth.

E. How has your child(ren) affected your sense of shared responsibility with your spouse? Check one.
   ❏ We are closer to each other as a result of parenting.
   ❏ We experience a lot of tension in our marriage about parenting.
   ❏ If anything, parenting has served to pull us apart.

Unfortunately, though, children can also act as a wedge in a marital relationship instead of as glue. George and Sandy worked during the first years of marriage and split the housework. Sandy did the cooking, and George did the housecleaning and laundry. When Sandy became pregnant, they agreed that she would work only part-time for a few years while this child, and maybe another child yet to come, were preschoolers. Since Sandy was home more with first one and then two children, she took on more of the housework. She also found that the children seemed to turn to her more often than George since she spent more time with them. She felt frustrated. Not only was she doing most of the housework that they had shared before, but the children also seemed to be her responsibility. George responded to Sandy's rising resentment by working harder and staying away from home even more. What had been a purpose that would be shared—rearing children—had become "Sandy's job."

F. Agree or disagree with each statement below by writing *A* or *D* before each.
   ___ Child rearing should be primarily Sandy's job.
   ___ Sandy's resentment is unfounded.
   ___ George is doing his part by earning a living for his family.
   ___ If Sandy goes back to work, George should again help around the house.
   ___ Sandy and George need to talk about what has happened and possibly realign responsibilities.

Many couples find themselves in the same situation Sandy and George faced. Parenting is supposed to be a job on the unity end of the balance; it is to be a shared commitment. But parenting often overburdens partners: there is not enough time to do all the housework, care for the children, and meet job responsibilities. Partners have to divide the load, each shouldering some of the burden. Sadly, many times the children become the responsibility of one partner while the other becomes the primary income earner. No wonder spouses sometimes feel as if their children pull them apart!

Children can provide their parents a sense of responsibility and commitment as they work together in behalf of their children

G. Identify one ongoing tension parenting has caused in your marriage.

_____

Name one action you could take that would decrease the tension arising from this issue.

_____

Parents are truly partners only if they share the responsibilities and joys of parenthood. Sometimes that may mean both parents sharing the same activities with their children. Other times that may mean one parent fixes and shares breakfast with the children and the other reads stories at bedtime. Whether working together or separately, though, partners need to feel shared commitment to the tasks of parenting.

H. Identify one task you do or did for your children that is or was primarily your responsibility.

_____

What one task has been or was primarily your mate's responsibility?

_____

We usually think of careers as being individual commitments, even though we support each other and are affected by each other's career in dramatic ways

Careers

When we talk about a sense of purpose in life, we also think about the career commitment each of us makes as individuals, whether it is to a paid job or homemaking. We usually think of careers as being individual commitments, even though we support each other and are affected by each other's career in dramatic ways. If parenting usually falls at the unity end of the pole, then careers fall at the individuality end. Nevertheless, it is possible for careers to be an arena for partnership. Some couples feel called into a career they share with each other—missionaries, teachers, writers, and farmers, for example.

I. If you and your mate are coworkers, check the phrase that describes the situation. If not, check the phrase that describes how you think you and your mate would function in the same workplace.
  - ❏ Mutually rewarding
  - ❏ The third world war
  - ❏ Harmonious
  - ❏ Walking on eggshells
  - ❏ You've got to be kidding!
  - ❏ Basically satisfying

Although for some it is possible, most spouses are not coworkers. Most spouses spend the majority of their weekdays apart, not working side by side. Not every purpose and commitment of our lives has to be shared; after all, individuality is an important balance to unity. It is important, however, for *both* partners to understand their relationship in the same way. If they are coworkers, then they both need to see their careers as shared. If they have individual careers, then both need to recognize that when it comes to their careers, they have made individual commitments that need support but do not depend on each other.

Mark was a corporate executive who traveled a great deal and was a key member of upper management. His wife, Gail, was not employed outside the home. She spent her days clearing the way for Mark to do his work. She planned elaborate dinner parties for his associates, handled his social-engagement calendar, and kept his closet full of suits dry-cleaned.

J. Would you describe Mark and Gail's relationship as a shared career, a partnership? ❏ Yes ❏ No ❏ Not sure

Perhaps the clearest way to determine whether a relationship is a shared career or partnership is to imagine each spouse's life without the other. If Gail died, even though Mark would grieve, his career would not be much affected. He might have to entertain in a restaurant instead of at home and carry his clothes to the cleaner himself, but he could manage. If Mark died, on the other hand, Gail's whole world would end. She would have no career to continue, for her whole career was being Mark's satellite.

Not all homemaking, however, requires being a satellite of the other spouse's career. Betty's husband worked with Mark in the same corporation. Betty did not work outside the home, but her life was full. She volunteered in a nearby nursing home, where she befriended several residents, whom she took on outings and involved in family activities. She also taught English-as-a-second-language classes at her church, and she linked the international persons she taught with church families who volunteered to provide friendship to these newcomers in the community.

Shared-career couples are not satellites of each other, either. Each contributes to his or her work together. Together they can do what neither could do alone. Even if they were separated by death, the remaining partner could continue their work, although probably not at the same level. Pat and Rick are both counselors. They work together in counseling families and have written several books together. Both of them could continue their work alone, although it would not have the same balance and quality their blended gifts make possible.

K. Identify your career commitment in your marriage by checking the best description.
❏ One has a career; the other is a satellite.
❏ One has a career, the other a life outside the relationship.
❏ Both have careers and are supportive of each other.
❏ Coworkers; careers are shared.
❏ Other: _____

The key, then, is for both partners to see their careers in the same way, whether at the pole of individuality or the pole of unity.

L. Find a time this week to talk to your mate about your careers. Are you comfortable with the way your careers are related to each other? Do you think your mate is comfortable with the present relationship?

Shared-career couples are not satellites of each other. Each contributes to his or her work together

Homemaking

Homemaking can refer to a career, as we discussed in the previous section. It includes all of the activities of operating a household and relating to the family's community. In fact, about the only clear definition of *homemaking* is that it is work without pay that occurs in or revolves around home and family.

We can talk about homemaking in another sense, however, that makes it a partnership, a shared commitment. Homemaking as an expression of partnership is "making a home." Homemaking includes all of the decisions a wife and a husband make together about how to spend their money, how to furnish their home, where to live, and when and whether others will be included in their home life.

What will your home stand for? Will it be simple or luxurious? Comfortable or formal? Clean or cluttered? With open or closed doors? A place to bring others into fellowship or a place to be alone together, sheltered from the world's hassles?

Homemaking, then, is not so much who washes dishes as it is deciding what mealtime will be like. Will it be a time when family members watch television and read a magazine or a time of conversation? A time to fill one's stomach as fast as possible in order to move to the next activity or a time to linger and enjoy one another's company? A time of privacy or a time to welcome others into the family circle?

Even if we give it no thought, the kinds of decisions we make about our shared home life and the patterns of relationships we develop have a purpose. That purpose may be to create a place of beauty, a place where family members can find rest and get away from the demands of hectic careers. Or it may be to create a comfortable place where friends and strangers can be found as often as the persons who actually live there.

The kinds of decisions we make about our shared home life and the patterns of relationships we develop have a purpose

M. Check the hymn titles that reflect your home's atmosphere and values.
- ❏ "It Is Well with My Soul"
- ❏ "The Fight Is On"
- ❏ "Abide with Me"
- ❏ "I Am a Stranger Here"
- ❏ "All Things Bright and Beautiful"
- ❏ "Haven of Rest"
- ❏ "Just as I Am"
- ❏ "Count Your Blessings"
- ❏ "Revive Us Again"

Whatever the style a couple chooses for their home, Christians are expected to practice hospitality.

N. Beside the Scripture references, paraphrase what the verses say about hospitality.

Romans 12:13: _____

1 Timothy 3:2: _____

Titus 1:8: _____

Hebrews 13:2: _____

1 Peter 4:9: _____

3 John 5-6: _____

Whatever style we choose for our home life, it needs to make strangers and friends feel welcome. One purpose of our life needs to be including others in our circle of love.

One of our fears is that if we get involved with others, we will not have time to nurture the intimacy so important in marriage. To practice hospitality, however, is not the same as keeping a busy social calendar, whirling from one dinner party to the next. True hospitality builds the intimacy of marriage, not detracts from it.

Mrs. Marlow lived next door to Micky and Susan. She was widowed, and her children lived in distant states. Over a period of months Micky, Susan, and Mrs. Marlow intentionally and increasingly opened their homes to each other. Several times a week they shared a meal. Mrs. Marlow on occasion helped them with child care so that Micky and Susan could have some time alone and the children could be with another adult who loved them. Micky and Susan helped Mrs. Marlow with some of the household repairs and yard work she would have had to pay for. Their growing relationship was a great strength in Micky and Susan's marriage and was a ministry to Mrs. Marlow.

O. Check the possibilities you and your family could begin that would encourage you to develop hospitality as a purpose for partnership.
❏ Sharing tools with neighbors
❏ Holding family clusters
❏ Becoming foster parents
❏ Inviting widows or widowers to dinner
❏ Entertaining new church members
❏ Having youth socials at your home
❏ Beginning a home Bible study
❏ Other: _____

Church and Community
Purpose for our lives, both as partners and as individuals, also comes from our relationships with our church and community. Covenant partners may choose ministry together, like Priscilla and Aquila, teaching or in other ways sharing a ministry in the church. You may also find a centering purpose for your shared life in the missions of the church or in the community beyond the life of the church. That may mean practicing hospitality in your home or becoming involved in the community, such as working to provide a playground or a recreational program for community children.

The World
Missions, world-hunger relief, peacemaking, and other global concerns can also be cores for partnership in marriage. You may hear God's call to serve by providing financial support and even become involved either by changing your lifestyle or by pursuing a career in a cause that is worth mutual commitment.

One of our fears is that if we get involved with others, we will not have time to nurture the intimacy so important in marriage

P. Fill in the chart for your marriage by giving a practical example in each category.

Arena	Joint Commitment	Individual Commitment
Parenting		
Careers		
Homemaking		
Church and community		
The world		

Each needs to recognize and support the other's gifts without having to be alike or even involved in order to communicate, "I'm behind you all the way."

THE PATTERNS OF RELATIONSHIP—A SECOND LOOK

As you look at the arenas of purpose mentioned in this lesson and think of others as well, it is clear that some purposes are shared and others are individual. A helpful exercise may be to expand exercise P and make a complete list of the centers of purpose in your life that are joint commitments and those that are individual.

Next, look back at the patterns in your relationship. Most likely, the patterns you have developed, such as unity versus individuality, probably fit the list you just made. If you seem to share many of your commitments, you are likely to be stronger in unity. If you have made many of your commitments individually, you are likely to be stronger in individuality.

Again, neither is necessarily better than the other. The important thing is that the relationship patterns fit the purposes that give shape to your life together. It creates conflict, for example, to have a purpose that calls for unity, like parenting, and yet handle the responsibility as though it were one individual's or the other's. Our patterns of relating need to help us achieve our purposes together, not hinder us. Different purposes require different patterns.

Q. Which pattern of relating does your chart in exercise P most reflect?
❏ Individuality ❏ Unity

Does your pattern of relating help you achieve your purposes together?
❏ Yes ❏ No

As we look at shared and individual purposes, we remember that, whether we are working together or supporting each other, difference and similarity need to be balanced. For example, if we have separate careers, there still needs to be similarity; we are enough alike to know about and appreciate what the other is doing. But there also needs to be difference; each needs to recognize and support the other's gifts without having to be alike or even involved in order to communicate, "I'm behind you all the way."

Covenant marriage involves each partner's supporting the other as an individual and each partner's committing to the partnership of shared purposes.

S. What is one purpose that is already a part of your relationship, or one you would like to add, to give special attention to during the coming week(s)?

What is one step you can take this week to raise this purpose to a place of importance in your relationship?

_____

SUMMARY

The aspect of covenant marriage we call partnership conveys the image of a husband and a wife standing shoulder to shoulder, facing a common work and calling together. Couples who share a common commitment find their partnerships becoming more intimate. Their marriages are strengthened as a result.

Shared goals and purposes can be found intentionally or unintentionally. Couples generally find purpose and meaning in their relationships with each other in five arenas: parenting, careers, homemaking, church and community, and the world.

Some of these purposes are joint commitments, while others are individual commitments. Different purposes require different patterns of relating. There needs to be a balance between unity and individuality and between difference and similarity.

Covenant marriage requires that each partner be committed to supporting the other partner in individual tasks and to working together in accomplishing shared responsibilities.

Covenant marriage requires that each partner be committed to supporting the other partner in individual tasks and to working together in accomplishing shared responsibilities

CHECKPOINT

The following review exercise is designed to reveal whether you have achieved the learning goals for lesson 6. Answer each question. Correct answers are given after the final question.

1. Which one of the following words or phrases capsules the best definition of *partnership* as it applies to marriage?
   ❑ a. Companions
   ❑ b. Sharing responsibilities
   ❑ c. On the same team
   ❑ d. Contributors
2. Which one of these is not an arena in which marriage operates as a partnership?
   ❑ a. Parenting
   ❑ b. Career
   ❑ c. Homemaking
   ❑ d. Personal hygiene
3. Identify one area in which you and your mate function as partners in—
   a. an activity we do together:

   _____

   b. an activity we do with others:

   _____

c. an activity we do for others:

_____

4. Identify one action you intend to take this week that will express your partnership in marriage.

_____

Now check your answers.
1. b
2. d
3. Personal response
4. Personal response

LOOKING AHEAD

Lesson 7 begins a new unit, "A Partnership of Equals," and deals with practical, nitty-gritty problems that often keep our marriage relationships from functioning as a covenant commitment.

Ask yourself: *What are the sources of anger and conflict in my marriage? What are the effects of anger and conflict on me, my mate, and our relationship?*

As a result of the next study, you will strengthen your ability to manage anger and conflict by reviewing what the Bible has to say and by developing new skills for coping with intense feelings.

UNIT 4

A PARTNERSHIP OF EQUALS

MANAGING ANGER AND CONFLICT

Lesson 7

An old adage says, "If you and your mate agree on everything, one of you is unnecessary"

LOOKING BACK

In unit 3 we were reminded that the exclusive, "I want to be with you all the time" kind of love experienced in early married life appropriately gives way to an expanded love that invites others to share the fruits of a couple's intimacy.

Christian couples should intentionally look for ways to practice servanthood through shared ministry. You were asked to identify shared purposes that were resulting in your working toward God's will for your marriage.

Did you discover ways you and your mate are functioning as partners? Did you decide on a ministry that would involve both of you in using your gifts? If you are already involved in an ongoing ministry, did you find ways you could work together more effectively? Becoming a strong team, pulling together to accomplish mutual goals, vividly demonstrates the difference Christ can make in a marriage.

OVERVIEW

An old adage says, "If you and your mate agree on everything, one of you is unnecessary." In my marriage both of us must be *very* necessary. We seem to have a different way of approaching almost everything.

What happens when marriage partners disagree? Is conflict a necessary part of marriage? How can you keep from getting so angry? These are some of the questions we will examine in this lesson. After we have identified the sources of conflict in marriage, we will look at constructive ways to handle them at home.

Think about how you handle conflict. Which strategy outlined in lesson 7 can help you manage anger and conflict more effectively?

When you complete this lesson, you will be able to—
• define *anger* and *conflict;*
• list six sources of anger and conflict;
• explain the effects of anger and conflict on you, on your mate, and on your relationship;
• summarize what the Bible says about anger and conflict;
• develop and demonstrate skills for managing anger and conflict;
• apply the skills you have learned in managing anger and conflict to your marriage this week.

SOURCES OF ANGER AND CONFLICT

No other relationship in our lives has as much potential for conflict as marriage. We share a car, our money, the kitchen, and a tube of toothpaste. Everywhere we turn, we run into each other's habits and quirks. We are expected to share values and goals and to live in basic agreement on both the big and little issues of life. And the expectations we bring to marriage are bound to clash with those of our partner in at least some respects. Whether it is the temperature to keep the house or whose family to visit at Christmas, conflict is inescapable in marriage.

Remember the differences that attracted you to each other that we discussed in lesson 4? Those same differences are often at the root of conflict spouses may experience in their relationship. Take, for example, the difference between the spouse who likes to plan ahead and the spouse who likes to do things on the spur of the moment. Susan wanted to plan the details of the weekend trip they had talked about. Burt, however, kept putting off talking about it: "Let's just do what we feel like doing. You can't schedule fun." Susan's frustration grew; for her, half the fun was thinking ahead about what they had planned and anticipating what they would do.

A. What is one difference between you and your spouse that has proved to be a source of conflict?

_____

_____

No other relationship in our lives has as much potential for conflict as marriage

Burt and Susan will probably not change their preferred styles of approaching leisuretime, but they must deal with the conflict their differences occasionally create. It is not the difference, then, but how that difference affects each of them that creates conflict. Differences become conflict when two persons are in a situation in which their differences unavoidably affect each other. If Burt and Susan were spending their weekend separately, their differences would not matter. When they spend it together, however, it will be difficult to avoid the conflict in their styles.

B. In your family of origin what differences between your parents seemed to result in conflict? How did they deal with those conflicts?

_____

_____

_____

A common response to marital conflict is anger. Yet it takes more than a conflict to create anger in one or both partners. Susan may react with anger when Burt puts her off for the fifth time when she asks him about the weekend. Or she may smile to herself and decide once again to plan it on her own and hope it works out. What makes the difference?

First, it depends on what else Susan is experiencing. If she is tired, tense from conflict with a neighbor or employer, or very excited about the weekend, she is more likely to get angry. Anger is a feeling, and it interacts with other feelings or body sensations we experience. The more tense or excited our bodies are for whatever reason, the more likely we are to get angry.

Second, it depends on what Susan thinks Burt's behavior means. If she interprets his behavior to mean how he feels about her, she is more likely to become angry. Susan may think to herself: *I'm not really important to him. He never takes my needs seriously. He doesn't understand how important this is to me; he's wrapped up in his own little world.* But if Susan interprets his behavior in another way that has little to do with her, she may be less likely to be angry. Then her thinking may be: *We are so different; he doesn't like to plan ahead. So many people at work have been demanding so much of him lately that it must be hard for him to feel pressured by me, too.* And it may be that Burt would give one, both, or neither of these interpretations in the same situation.

Conflict, then, is the result of two persons' differences; it belongs to the relationship. Anger is the response of one or both partners to the conflict, to the other tension or excitement being felt, and to the interpretation the angry person gives to the conflict. One person cannot make another angry, because one cannot control another person's feelings and thoughts. Both partners are responsible for their own feelings. Both are responsible for finding ways to deal with their differences and conflicts that build rather than destroy their intimacy with each other.

C. Look back at your response to exercise A. How could thinking about the two considerations mentioned above help you not become angry?

_____

_____

Spouses find themselves in conflict and becoming angry with each other for a variety of reasons.

Behaviors that inconvenience and irritate. Behaviors that can create feelings of anger because they inconvenience or irritate include personal habits (finger chewing, personal grooming at home, or reading the paper at the table), household living behaviors (leaving the toilet seat up, waiting a week to take out the garbage, or leaving dirty dishes on the table), and personal styles (being an early riser who likes to bounce out of bed at 6:00 a.m. or being a night owl who likes to sleep late).

These behaviors seem insignificant, but like a splinter in your thumb, they irritate and distract, pulling attention away from significant issues to this worrisome little pain. To someone else it seems so minor, but when it's your thumb, no splinter is easy to ignore. In the same way, minor annoyances in marriage may distract us from other issues and absorb major portions of our relationship with each other. They persistently jab us because we experience them day in and day out.

Behaviors that indicate basic value differences. Both spouses have dreams and goals, both for them as individuals and for their marriage. Individual goals might include building financial security or using money to bring pleasure to others or themselves without worrying about the future. They may

> *Both partners are responsible for their own feelings. Both are responsible for finding ways to deal with their differences and conflicts that build rather than destroy their intimacy with each other*

have always wanted to travel, or they may have wanted to be able to relax at a nearby lake without the hassle of planning trips.

Our expectations of marriage may also conflict. One partner believes that spouses ought to share all of their activities with each other, discontinue friendships that do not include the partner, touch each other affectionately and often, and hold hands walking down the street. The other spouse may believe that partners ought to support and encourage each other but not try to control each other and ought to reserve displays of affection for private moments.

Often we do not even realize we have these values, these oughts, until they clash with our partner's. They seem like the right way to do things—until they collide head-on with the partner's right way.

Conflicts over style. The four styles of relating in marriage—individuality and unity, similarity and difference—provide fertile ground for conflict. One style is not better than another, nor should spouses choose one style or another and stick to it. Marriages need all four styles of relating.

Spouses experience conflict, however, when one spouse tackles a problem or a task using one style and the other tackles it using another. One spouse wants to divide the task and each do what they do best—a style emphasizing difference ("You grocery shop, and I'll clean the house")—while the other wants each person's part to equal the other's—emphasizing similarity ("I'll grocery shop this time, but you have to do it next time").

D. **List one of your attributes in each of the following categories that your mate has identified as a source of conflict.**

Personal habit: _____

Household living behavior: _____

Value difference: _____

Personal style: _____

What have you done in each instance to try to lessen these potential sources of conflict?

Frustration and tension from other sources. Tension in marriage often results from anger we experience but choose not to express in other relationships. Instead of telling the boss, the work colleague, or the store clerk our feelings, we remain tense and upset because our work has been unjustly criticized, our colleague has borrowed and marked up our work manual, or the store clerk has embarrassed us.

Tension can also result when physical objects frustrate us—a stuck zipper when we are in a hurry, a car that will not start, and a map that is no help in a strange city. Often the spouse gets the brunt of our frustration.

A stray look or saying or doing the wrong thing by our spouse is all it takes for our anger to take shape when we are already tense, upset, tired, sick, or excited. We may then find ourselves blaming the partner for all we are feeling. By blaming our partner, we do not have to take any responsibility for the problem; it's all the partner's fault.

Tension in marriage often results from anger we experience but choose not to express in other relationships

93

The Letter of James instructs us to be "slow to anger, for the anger of man does not work the righteousness of God" (James 1:19-20, RSV). Conflict needs to be thought about and mulled over, not hastily expressed in anger. Reflecting on and determining the source of our frustration and irritation before we respond to our partner in anger is helpful. How much of what we are feeling is generated by the conflict between us? How have I interpreted the conflict? And how much of the intensity of what I am feeling comes from sources of tension other than our relationship?

E. **What are some of the sources of tension you find creeping into your feelings about your mate?**
   - ❑ Your boss
   - ❑ Work colleagues
   - ❑ Being late
   - ❑ Traffic jams
   - ❑ The weather
   - ❑ Relatives
   - ❑ Financial worries
   - ❑ Problems with the kids
   - ❑ Church squabbles
   - ❑ How you feel (health concerns)

Concern for each other. Sometimes even our concern for each other creates conflict. To listen to each other's hurts and troubles and not want to do something to make things better for our cherished partner is sometimes difficult.

Perhaps we want our partner to listen to our advice, which we think will help the situation, advice that conflicts with the partner's style of handling difficulties. Since the hurting partner is already tense and upset, the potential for anger is there. When we respond with concern and worry about our partner, our own tension and potential for anger rise. We both want a resolution of the difficulty but disagree about how to get it.

Jim complained to Judy about a nagging cold and fatigue. He felt sick for weeks and could not seem to shake it. Judy responded: "You just don't take care of yourself. If you would just quit working so hard and go to bed for a few days, you could lick it. What makes you think the world can't go on without you?"

Judy was genuinely concerned about Jim; his illness worried her, and she thought her advice ought to help. Jim, however, felt misunderstood and attacked rather than getting longed-for sympathy and praise for his hard work despite feeling sick. Both felt angry after their exchange.

To be frustrated with a virus, with work that needs to be done, with a sick spouse is easy to understand. But it is easy to transform that frustration into anger at a spouse who does not take care of himself and then complains when he gets sick or at a spouse who is cruelly unsympathetic with her partner's heavy burden.

F. **Label each of the following concerns M for *me* if it is a worry your mate has expressed about you or H for *him* or *her* if it is a worry you have about your mate.**
   ___ Is overweight
   ___ Is underweight

Conflict needs to be thought about and mulled over, not hastily expressed in anger

___ Eats junk food
___ Skips meals
___ Doesn't get enough exercise
___ Doesn't get enough sleep
___ Spends too much time watching TV
___ Is overworked
___ Is underpaid
___ Is frequently sick

Look at the list you labeled *H*. If your spouse expressed his or her concern the way you have, would the situation be better or worse?

All of the above. Sometimes our conflicts with each other clearly fall into one or another of these categories. Other times, however, it depends on how you look at it; they may all be involved in some way or another.

The sick husband and his wife in the previous section were certainly in conflict over concern for each other. More than likely, other issues were involved as well. She was also tired from a hard day of work; her feet hurt, and the thought of fixing dinner seemed overwhelming. She was looking at a clutter of newspapers, clothing, and tools her husband had left on the dining table; she has asked repeatedly that he put his things away and not leave them all over the house. But it is hard to ask him to do things when he is not well. And now he is complaining about feeling sick and having too much work, when the weekend she had looked forward to for more than a year, when they were to leave the children with a sitter and be together alone, is just three days away.

What is the real issue here? The answer, of course, is that they are all real issues. The situation will require delineating the different strands of conflict if this couple is able to deal with their anger constructively.

G. Answer *T* for *true* or *F* for *false*.
When I am angry at my mate—
___ there is usually more than one reason;
___ it's usually because I'm in a bad mood;
___ it's due to my concern for him or her;
___ other sources of tension contribute to it;
___ it's generally something minor;
___ it's generally something major.

WHAT SPOUSES DO WITH ANGER
What do you do when you are angry with each other? All partners get angry on occasion, but we have different strategies for handling our feelings. Two strategies do more damage than any other, ventilating and withdrawing.

Ventilating
Ventilating anger means letting it out, much like the vent in a volcano that lets out the building steam and smoke. Ventilating does nothing to change what is causing the steam and smoke in the first place; it merely lets out the hot air that is accumulating. Ventilating anger includes shouting, throwing things, making quiet but devastating remarks, calling names, using hostile humor, and attacking physically or verbally.

Ventilating anger includes shouting, throwing things, making quiet but devastating remarks, calling names, using hostile humor, and attacking physically or verbally

95

Because ventilating supposedly reduces the pressure inside, people have the idea that it gets rid of or lessens the anger. If anything, however, ventilating anger actually increases anger. The focus is on self-expression, and the more we talk about our feelings, often the more intensely we feel them. In addition, the attack on our spouse is often met with counterattack, which generates even more anger. Dealing with the conflict between us in any constructive way when we have been blasting each other with the heat of anger is often difficult.

Ventilating lets anger, not love, take over. When we respond to each other without thinking, ventilating is often the result, and the results are often not what we would choose.

The Bible describes many occasions when anger took the form of ventilating, including physical assault and verbal hostility, which led to disaster (see Genesis 49:5-7; Exodus 2:11-15; 2 Samuel 13). Ventilating anger leads inevitably to trouble (see Proverbs 14:17,29; Ecclesiastes 7:9). Jesus equated anger that results in insults and name calling ("You fool!") with murder (see Matthew 5:22, RSV). By reducing another person to an object, to a name, we have in essence killed the person by denigrating his or her personhood. The saying "Sticks and stones may break my bones, but words can never hurt me" is far from the truth.

Ephesians 4:26, "Be angry but do not sin" (RSV), has often been misinterpreted to mean that it is all right to be angry as long as we do not sin in our anger. But a better interpretation is "If you are angry, do not let anger lead you into sin" (NEB). Anger is dangerous; it is a loophole for the devil if we allow it to remain in us over time while we righteously savor the injustice done to us and think about how to get even (see Ephesians 4:26-27, RSV). Anger needs to be carefully considered, not hastily vented, and then it needs to be expressed in a way that allows us to work together to resolve the conflict between us, not allowed to grow inside us and feed plans for getting even.

H. Explain in your own words why ventilation is a damaging way to handle anger.

_____

_____

Withdrawing

The opposite of ventilating is withdrawing. Instead of expressing the anger openly, we hide it and pull away from our partner to avoid having to deal with whatever has made us angry. We may bury ourselves in our work or the TV or the Internet, give our partner the silent treatment, refuse to talk about it and engage in only trivial conversation, or leave.

Unfortunately, the effects are almost the same as those of ventilating. The conflict that created the anger in the first place gets ignored, and our withdrawing from the partner increases the chances that the partner will also become angry. For the partner, our withdrawing often feels like being tried and condemned for a wrongdoing without even being able to discuss it.

Fortunately, ways other than ventilating and withdrawing are more effective in handling conflict and anger. They include postponing, reinterpreting, and facing the issue.

Withdrawing from the partner increases the chances that the partner will also become angry

Postponing

One of the most important choices we can make is to wait to express our anger and to deal with the conflict between us at an appropriate time and place, "as fits the occasion" (Ephesians 4:29, RSV). To express anger hastily is foolish (see Proverbs 14:17,29; Ecclesiastes 7:9); we often need to take time to sort out what we are feeling, what we want to say to our partner, and how we want to say it.

Postponing is not the same as withdrawing. We often need to say to each other: "I'm upset [angry, frustrated, mad], and I need some time to think about this. Let me have until after supper, and then let's sit down and talk." Any time and place will do, as long as each of you can give the issue your attention without other distractions, tensions, or fatigue. For example, just before bedtime, when both are tired, may be the worst time for many couples.

I. When is usually not a good time to talk with your spouse?

_____

When is usually a good time to talk with your spouse?

_____

The Scripture says, "Do not let the sun go down on your anger" (Ephesians 4:26, RSV). Some have misunderstood this to mean that all conflict needs to be resolved before the day ends. The new Jewish day began at sundown. The Bible here is reminding us not to drag out our anger and let it affect our future with each other but to deal with it and move on. The Scripture verse does not mean that we need to have marathon sessions of trying to resolve conflict before sleeping. We need to be sensitive to each other's needs, moods, and abilities to deal with problems. We need to deal with anger as soon as fits the occasion, but not with a bedtime deadline like high noon in a Hollywood Western.

J. How should you act toward your mate while you are waiting for an appropriate moment to talk? Check one.
- ❏ Pout
- ❏ Silent treatment
- ❏ Martyred look
- ❏ Angry
- ❏ Concerned
- ❏ As if nothing has happened

Other times we may decide to say nothing to our partner about a conflict or our anger because we are sensitive to the partner's needs. When a partner is stressed by other demands, tired, sick, or depressed, it is probably not the best time to talk about problems and anger. A better approach is to make a silent contract with ourselves to bring it up at a more opportune time; there is "a time to keep silence, and a time to speak" (Ecclesiastes 3:7, RSV). We are not withdrawing from our feelings and the conflict but deciding to handle them at a fit occasion (see Ephesians 4:29).

> *When a partner is stressed by other demands, tired, sick, or depressed, it is probably not the best time to talk about problems and anger*

Sometimes we also need to postpone conflict and anger until we have had time to sift through what we are feeling and choose what our goals will be. Do I want to insult my partner, blame my partner, and make myself look like the victim of my partner's insensitivity? Or do I want to communicate my feelings in such a way that we both can tackle the conflict and strengthen our relationship? We can decide how to communicate even anger.

Postponing anger can help us change "You jerk! Don't you ever think about anyone but yourself?" to "I am furious that you left me standing on the street corner for an hour because you got distracted. I feel unimportant to you, and I want to be important in your life. And I want you to stick to what you say you will do."

K. Which of the following reasons suggests why you insist on settling a conflict immediately?
   ❑ You want to get your feelings off your chest and be finished with the situation.
   ❑ You want to strengthen your relationship by communicating your feelings in a loving way.

Reinterpreting

When you are angry, take time to think before acting or talking

When you are angry, take time to think before acting or talking. First, rerun the tape of what has happened and separate what you observed from what you think it meant, as best as possible. For example, I am angry because my partner has once again washed all of the dishes but left the pots and pans and the dirty stove for me to clean. What I observe is dirty pots and pans left on the stove. What I think it means is that my partner left the dirtiest work for me because my partner thought that his or her time and energy were more important than mine.

But the situation might have another interpretation. I might look at the same pots and pans and become alarmed, wondering what has happened that caused my partner to stop in the middle of the job. Perhaps one of the children got hurt, or my partner was distracted by another crisis. Or perhaps my partner did not leave them for me but instead is planning to come back and finish the job after tending to a more urgent task. The same conflict is there, but I no longer feel angry as much as I feel concerned or worried.

L. Read the following case study. List possible interpretations of this event that would not make Donald the guilty party.

Becky hurriedly unlocked the door, set her bag of groceries on the kitchen counter, and picked up the ringing phone. The call was the child-care director saying that no one had picked up her children. *Donald promised to pick up the kids today so that I could get groceries,* Becky thought. She told the director she'd be right over and apologized for the delay. "If Donald forgot what he promised me, I'll kill him!" Becky screamed as she grabbed her keys and ran to the car.

_____

_____

One way to interpret a conflict is to place myself behind my partner's eyes. What does my partner see and feel about what has happened? My view and my partner's view may be quite different, each just as right as the other. The key is not who is right or wrong but how can we understand each other's perspective better so that we can deal most effectively with the difference between us.

Reinterpretation, then, means asking ourselves three questions:

1. Can I separate what I observed or experienced from what I think it means?
2. What else may what I observed or experienced mean, especially from my spouse's perspective?
3. What other factors (tension, fatigue, other issues) are complicating my view of the situation?

M. Use the three previous questions to rethink a recent conflict you had with your spouse. Would the situation have turned out different if you had asked these questions at the time? ❑ Yes ❑ No

Facing the Issue

Finally, of course, comes the time to say to my partner, "I am angry!" To be most effective, I need to define the situation in such a way that together we can focus on what we can do about it. "You are a slob" is not facing the issue; it is ventilating. That kind of response makes my partner defensive and less willing to think about changes; in fact, it does not even indicate what kind of change is desired. "I am angry when I find your clothes all over the bathroom, because I work hard to keep this place clean" is more likely to be met with a listening ear and the possibility of change.

Three pieces need to be included in facing the issue:

1. I feel (angry, hurt, ignored) ...
2. when you (whatever has happened) ...
3. because (the value or belief challenged by what has happened).

Certainly, we do not need to use the formula words "I feel ... when you ... because..." every time we want to talk with our spouse about anger or conflict. But whatever your style, all three elements need to be communicated in some way. First, tell your partner what you are feeling. Second, state what has happened—what you saw or heard or felt that you associate with the feelings. And third, state how what has happened conflicts with what you want. By sharing our feelings this way, we have a firm foundation for tackling our differences in a way that is edifying and that imparts grace (see Ephesians 4:29).

O. What is the formula that helps us face the issue?
❑ You make me ... when you ... because ...
❑ I feel ... when you ... because ...

What is the difference between these two formulas?

The key is not who is right or wrong but how can we understand each other's perspective better so that we can deal most effectively with the difference between us

Ephesians 4:15,25-32 gives helpful suggestions for sharing our feelings and facing our conflict together.

P. Read Ephesians 4:15,25-32 in more than one translation, if possible, before you proceed to the next paragraph. A helpful discipline is to underline verses in your Bible that you find meaningful for quick reference in the future. You may want to underline these verses.

Speak the truth in love. We are not to ventilate our anger in hateful ways, nor are we to avoid the truth of hurt feelings and conflict that alienates us from each other. Instead, we need to face the truth of our conflict, our differences in loving ways that respect the viewpoints and needs of both of us. Avoid exaggerating or embellishing the facts to justify yourself or make the other person feel guilty. Avoid words like *always* and *never.* They are unlikely to be true and are likely to expand the conflict, adding more heat than light to the issue.

Impart grace. Share anger in ways that can be experienced as good and helpful for the partner. Focus on your observations—what you've seen or heard—not on your partner's personhood. Comment on what the partner did (or did not do) or said (or did not say); do not jump to character judgments about who your partner is (a jerk, thoughtless, irresponsible). Attack your problem, not each other.

Let no evil talk come from your mouths but only that which edifies. Anger always needs to be channeled and controlled; it has power that is to be used to strengthen our love and commitment to each other, not to destroy each other. Keep the focus on strengthening the relationship by resolving the conflict, not on winning a victory over the partner.

Choose an appropriate time and place. Learn when and where each is strongest and can give his or her best to the task of dealing with feelings and problems; do not shortchange the relationship by giving it only leftover moments of time and energy for necessary maintenance.

Do not let the sun go down on your anger. Postpone anger only if you commit yourself to deal with it at a specific time; do not hold on to it indefinitely, nursing it and giving it a life of its own. Deal with it as soon as a "fit occasion" arises and then let go of it. "Let all bitterness and wrath and anger and clamor and slander be put away from you, with all malice, and be kind to one another, tenderhearted, forgiving one another, as God in Christ forgave you" (Ephesians 4:31-32, RSV).

Q. What have you learned about managing anger and conflict that you want to implement in your marriage relationship this week? Write two ideas.

1. _____

2. _____

SUMMARY

Conflict is to be expected when two persons share the same living space. Almost every decision by one person affects the other. A number of sources of conflict exist in a marriage. Some of these sources are behaviors that inconve-

---

Keep the focus on strengthening the relationship by resolving the conflict, not on winning a victory over the partner

nience and irritate, behaviors that indicate basic value differences, conflicts over style, frustration and tension from other sources, and concern for each other. Sometimes one of these factors produces conflict, but most of the time all of them are involved.

Marriage partners may choose to respond to conflict either positively or negatively. Two negative ways of managing conflict are ventilating (letting it out without regard for timing or the feelings of the other) and withdrawing (pulling away from our partner to avoid having to deal with whatever has made us angry).

The good news is that conflict does not have to result in anger. Three better ways of coping with conflict are postponing the confrontation until an appropriate time, reinterpreting the conflict instead of assessing blame, and facing the issues. The principles laid down in Ephesians 4:15,25-32 remind us to speak the truth in love.

Speak the truth in love

CHECKPOINT

The following review exercise is designed to reveal whether you have achieved the learning goals for lesson 7. Answer each question. Correct answers are given after the final question.

1. Write *T* for *true* or *F* for *false*.

___ a. Marriage has more potential for conflict than any other relationship.

___ b. Individual differences are the root of conflict in marriage.

___ c. Marriage partners should not be irritated by their mates' personal habits or styles.

___ d. When partners disagree over a value judgment, they should decide which is the right way and go with it.

___ e. Frustration and tension from other sources are often unfairly attributed to the spouse.

___ f. Partners may get angry with each other because of their concern for each other.

2. List two ways to deal with anger that damage a relationship.

a. _____

b. _____

3. Which one of the following ways is the best way to deal with anger?
  ❑ a. Postponing
  ❑ b. Reinterpreting
  ❑ c. Facing the issue
  ❑ d. All of the above

4. Match each of the following Scripture verses with a summary statement.
  ___ a. James 1:19b-20   (1) Don't let anger lead you into sin.
  ___ b. Ephesians 4:26   (2) There is a time to keep silent.
  ___ c. Ecclesiastes 3:7b   (3) Be slow to anger.
  ___ d. Ephesians 4:32   (4) Be kind to one another.
                             (5) To express anger hastily is foolish.

Now check your answers.
1. a. *T*, b. *T*, c. *F*, d. *F*, e. *T*, f. *T*
2. a. ventilating, b. withdrawing
3. d
4. a. (3), b. (1), c. (2), d. (4)

LOOKING AHEAD

How do you and your partner make decisions? Do you make most decisions, or does your mate? Do you have certain turfs that determine who decides what is best in each area of family life? Do both of you try to make every decision together?

Lesson 8 will help you develop and demonstrate skills in making decisions and resolving conflict. The lesson will enable you to overcome or eliminate common difficulties associated with decision making.

As you go through your week, think about the how and who of decision making in your home.

MAKING DECISIONS AND RESOLVING CONFLICT

Lesson 8

LOOKING BACK

Lesson 7 helped us understand why conflict is inherent in marriage, even in covenant marriage. We looked at sources of conflict between partners. As you think about a recent conflict in your home, can you pinpoint why you felt as you did? What factors contributed to your feelings?

We have the choice to respond to our feelings either positively or negatively. The good news is that conflict in marriage does not have to result in anger. We have better ways of coping with conflict than ventilating anger or withdrawing from our partner.

Can you recall the three positive approaches to dealing with conflict outlined in lesson 7? If not, review them before you continue.

OVERVIEW

Is it possible for two persons to enter a conflict and both come out winners? In this lesson you will learn how you and your mate can develop skills in decision making that will result in a win-win situation.

We will look at five relationship issues that can prevent couples from being winners. Then we will examine four ways couples make decisions. We will identify a biblical model that will enable you to solve problems in a more productive manner.

Before you begin, write on a separate sheet of paper how you and your partner make decisions. How does your method work for you? Determine to find in this lesson at least one new skill you can apply to decision making in your marriage.

When you complete this lesson, you will be able to—
- define *decision making* and *problem solving;*
- describe four ways people make decisions and solve problems;
- identify five difficulties in decision making and problem solving;
- summarize what the Bible says about decision making and problem solving;
- develop and demonstrate skills for making decisions and solving problems;
- apply the skills you have learned to problems or decisions that arise in your marriage this week.

CHANGE REQUIRES DECISION MAKING
Susan: I am really angry! I thought we agreed that each of us would watch our spending until we get out of this financial hole. But I just looked at the check-

book, and you wrote a check for more than two hundred dollars for new clothes! I've been doing without, but that apparently doesn't matter to you. I feel cheated, and I feel that my needs aren't as important as yours.

Patrick: So from your perspective I've been unfair, and that says to you that I don't care as much about what you need as about what I need.

Susan: That's right!

Patrick: That's not what I meant to do at all. I just found a great sale, and I hated not to get things I would spend more for if I waited. I thought I was living up to our agreement by being careful. I'm a little hurt that you would question my judgment; I still think I made a good decision.

A. Check the source of conflict in this case study.
❑ Irritation or inconvenience
❑ Value difference
❑ Style
❑ Frustration and tension from other sources
❑ Concern for each other

Check the strategy Susan used in managing her anger.
❑ Ventilating
❑ Withdrawing
❑ Postponing
❑ Reinterpreting
❑ Facing the issue

> *Spouses must decide how they will live with conflicts in their personalities, styles of living, and values*

Where do Patrick and Susan go from here? They have expressed feelings to each other by offering them as their own reactions to the issue. They have recognized their value difference, faced the issue, and reported their own perspectives on what happened. Neither insulted the other or assumed that the partner would see it the same way. Even though they may understand each other at this point, conflict still exists between them.

B. What might happen if Susan and Patrick choose to drop the subject and forget about it? Check your choices.
❑ The matter will go away and never come back.
❑ Susan will bring up the subject again.
❑ Patrick will bring up the subject again.
❑ Something will happen that will cause the subject to resurface.
❑ Susan might not say anything, but inside she will still be angry at Patrick.
❑ Patrick might not say anything, but inside he will continue to feel hurt by Susan's words.

Often, understanding each other is not enough. Spouses must decide how they will live with conflicts in their personalities, styles of living, and values.

C. What would you advise Susan and Patrick to do to try to resolve the conflict between them?
❑ Return the clothes to the store.
❑ Let Susan spend a comparable sum of money on things she needs.

❏ Susan should agree with Patrick's actions.
❏ Patrick should admit that he used bad judgment.
❏ Other: _____

If these personal conflicts were all spouses had to deal with, eventually they might come up with workable solutions to all of their differences and would face no more conflict. But any veteran of a long marriage knows that the possibilities for conflict keep developing in marriage. Spouses change, and the world around them changes. Many of these changes require partners to adjust and make new decisions. Daily spouses are confronted with decisions because of changes in their environment, new ideas, and changes within each of the individual partners.

D. Name one change that has occurred during the past year in—

your mate: _____

your ideas: _____

your environment: _____

Partners make many of these decisions without giving them a second thought. They have had enough experiences responding to changes and crises that everyone knows what to do. When little Peggy brought home a bad report card, partners acted. Mom called the teacher to schedule an appointment, Dad began to monitor homework, and both began to monitor Peggy's TV viewing and sleep habits more closely. They may never have had to deal with a bad report card before, but in this family Mom was almost always the one who contacted people outside the family, and Dad was almost always the one who worked with the children on their school work. Both parents thought that TV viewing needed to be kept to a minimum and that children needed scheduled bedtimes to do their best in school.

However, other aspects of the problem faced them that required face-to-face discussion and difficult decisions. In the conference Mom scheduled, the teacher suggested that Peggy seemed to be struggling to keep up with the other children; the problem was not just Peggy's failing to do her homework or not getting enough sleep. The teacher said she would like to keep Peggy back in the same grade. Mom tended to agree with the teacher, but Dad thought that with special tutoring and their support and encouragement, Peggy could do better if she stayed with her age group.

E. If this problem occurred in your household and both partners did not agree, how would you handle the conflict? Check one.
❏ Keep talking until we reach consensus.
❏ Probably go with Mom's viewpoint.
❏ Probably go with Dad's viewpoint.
❏ Let the teacher decide.
❏ Draw straws.
❏ Other: _____

Daily spouses are confronted with decisions because of changes in their environment, new ideas, and changes within each of the individual partners

105

This conflict came to the surface as a result of being parents, changes in their family environment (having a daughter in school), and ideas and beliefs (that their child might not be capable of *A* schoolwork). It was a conflict that required decision making, just as the difference in values about money did for Susan and Patrick.

Here are some examples of the kinds of changes couples confront that require decision making. As you look through this list, perhaps you will remember similar decisions you and your partner have faced or face now.

F. Check any of the following changes you have confronted in the past year. Write *X* beside the changes you are still dealing with.

Changes in Environment
❑ A major appliance that required repair or replacement
❑ Job promotion that required moving
❑ Problems with neighbors or extended family
❑ Storm damage to property
❑ Child's illness (who stays home?)
❑ Financial crisis (what cuts to make?)
❑ Elder care

New Ideas
❑ An article about how to have greater intimacy in marriage
❑ Going online and subscribing to particular Web sites
❑ Computerizing home finances
❑ Satellite dish and staying home to watch movies instead of going out
❑ Lifestyle changes in nutrition and healthful eating
❑ Changing roles of men and women
❑ This marriage-enrichment group
❑ Time-share investments
❑ Reducing expenses to allow Mom to stay at home

Changes in Individuals
❑ One partner losing 50 pounds and feeling more attractive and energetic
❑ Illness or injury
❑ Pregnancy and nursing
❑ Mid-life changes
❑ Religious conversion and faith development

When we think about it, our marriage is under a constant barrage of changes from around us and inside us to which our relationship must constantly adjust. Many of these adjustments simply happen without our giving much thought or discussion to them. But many others require extended conversations and serious decision making. As you look back at your past together as a couple and consider decisions successfully made, there is much to celebrate!

G. Identify one change you checked in exercise F. How did it affect your marriage?

Our marriage is under a constant barrage of changes from around us and inside us to which our relationship must constantly adjust

What was the outcome?

_____

_____

Are you pleased with the way the change was handled? ❑ Yes ❑ No

ISSUES IN CONFLICT RESOLUTION AND DECISION MAKING
Many times the changes from outside our marriage are further complicated by the differences between partners. Little Peggy's problems in school required decisions by her parents. Those decisions were complicated by the fact that her father highly valued school achievement and was determined that his children would do well. Mom, on the other hand, wanted them to do well but thought there was more to life than school achievement. She was most concerned that her children were happy and satisfied with themselves.

So not only are spouses confronted daily with change from the outside, but they must also live with a myriad of differences between them in their values and beliefs, differences that turn change into marital conflict. Few of us are even aware of the many problems and marital conflicts we have successfully faced together. We are usually more aware of the unresolved conflict facing us today than those we have successfully faced in the past. Read the following list of common marital conflicts. How many of these issues have created conflict at some time in your marriage? How have you resolved the conflict? Which ones still create conflict?

H. Check the appropriate column to indicate the degree to which the issues in the following list of marital conflicts have affected your marriage.

Many times the changes from outside our marriage are further complicated by the differences between partners

	Not an Issue	Resolved	Still an Issue
Money			
1. Whether to spend or save			
2. How to spend			
3. How to save			
4. Whether to buy expensive things that last or inexpensive things that may not last			
5. Whether or not to use credit			
Employment			
1. Whether one or both should work outside the home			
2. Expectations of each to be involved in the other's career			
3. Whether to move for job-related reasons			
4. Whether to let work time interfere with family time			
Home Responsibilities			
1. Who cleans, cooks, launders			
2. Who repairs, oversees repair persons			
3. How to decorate and furnish our home			
4. How to entertain company			
5. Who writes letters, sends Christmas cards, pays bills			

107

	Not an Issue	Resolved	Still an Issue

Sexual and Emotional Intimacy
1. What kind of birth control, if any, is used
2. When and how to be sexually intimate
3. Where to be sexually intimate
4. When to be alone together
5. How to express feelings
6. How to show love

Children
1. Whether to have children
2. How to discipline
3. What kind of care or education to give children
4. Who cares for children at what times
5. What expectations to have of children

Extended Family and Friends
1. How much time and energy to spend with them
2. How to support and care for them
3. Whether to ask for help from them
4. How much to tell them about our private lives

Church and Faith
1. Which church?
2. The role of church in our lives
3. Whether and how to have family worship
4. How much time and money to give
5. The role of faith in our relationship

Leisuretime
1. How to spend leisuretime
2. Where to go on vacation
3. Whether to have individual or shared activities

Sometimes decision making and conflict resolution seem more difficult than they ought to, given the size of the problem

As you look together at the conflicts and problems you have faced together, even though there may be some that continue to call for decisions, many have been successfully resolved. And even though we need to work on the problems still before us, we also need a time to celebrate together what we have done. Then we have more energy and hope to face the conflicts yet before us.

Sometimes decision making and conflict resolution seem more difficult than they ought to, given the size of the problem. Have you and your partner ever argued for hours (or days) about something that seemed unimportant, except that it generated so much anger? Such issues are often lightning rods for another agenda in the marriage. We want to resolve the conflict, but we want to resolve it in such a way that one of the following results.

1. I win and feel superior. (I know much more than you about this. Just let me handle it.)
2. My partner is blamed for the problem, and I don't have to accept any responsibility for it. (It's all your fault that she's failing in school. You never spend any time with her. I've certainly done everything I can.)
3. I get my partner's attention. (I'll get you to listen to me even if I have to irritate you by making mountains out of mole hills.)
4. I am martyred; my partner wins but feels guilty. (You win; I am willing to sacrifice my needs for yours. See what a good spouse I am?)

5. I don't have any part in making the decision, so whatever happens will be my partner's fault. (You decide where we will eat out, and if the food is bad, you will have no one to blame but yourself.)

I. Number each statement with the number corresponding to the type of conflict resolution previously listed.
  ___ a. "Why did you shower in my tub? You use the front bath, remember? You are so inconsiderate."
  ___ b. "All right. We'll go to your mother's. My parents will just have to understand."
  ___ c. "I've been there before. I'll drive."
  ___ d. "What do you want me to wear? They are your friends."
  ___ e. "If you would paddle her, she wouldn't get into your flowers!"
  Answers: a. 3, b. 4, c. 1, d. 5, e. 2

When any of these issues are involved, they are likely to play a more important role in the conflict than the actual issue that started the conflict, such as where to eat dinner. The issue is not so much where we eat but how we decide. This is because how we decide touches off a relationship concern.

The previous list reflects personal needs of which we are probably only half aware. Although they create problems in marriage and often interfere with intimacy and communication, we need to recognize what those needs are. When they are out in the open, we can work on them together instead of allow them to develop into sneaky tactics that get in the way of good decision making.

Some of the needs behind these conflicts are listed below. These are only suggestions; you will need to decide if they are accurate in your relationship.
1. Superiority—I need to feel important and valued by you.
2. Blaming—I am afraid of letting you see me as imperfect and of having to face myself as imperfect.
3. Attention—I need something from you, but I don't know how to ask or even what it is.
4. Martyrdom—I want to feel like a good spouse who does whatever I can for you, but I become resentful that you don't do the same for me.
5. Refusing to decide—I am afraid of taking responsibility for our decisions because you might get angry if they don't work well, and I don't want to face your anger. It is easier to blame you than to share the responsibility.

J. Rate the extent to which these feelings are reflected in your relationship with your mate. 1 = does not apply, 2 = applies somewhat, 3 = applies, 4 = applies to a great extent.
  Superiority   1 2 3 4
  Blaming   1 2 3 4
  Attention   1 2 3 4
  Martyrdom   1 2 3 4
  Refusing to decide   1 2 3 4

Total your scores for 1 and 3. A score of 6 or higher indicates a need to control the relationship. Total your scores for 2, 4, and 5. A score of 9 or more indicates a need to be controlled.

When personal needs are out in the open, we can work on them together instead of allow them to develop into sneaky tactics that get in the way of good decision making

These are not easy issues to resolve, but when we talk about them, we share important needs and longings with each other. The skills of conflict resolution presented later in this lesson can be helpful as we work on these issues together.

PATTERNS OF DECISION MAKING

Decision making can be defined as any activity or conversation that results in a couple's deciding what they will do or say in response to a change from within or without or to an issue that creates conflict between them. Couples make decisions in four ways.

Autocratic Decision Making

One person makes the decisions, and the other follows. Even though conflict is kept to a minimum, autocratic decision making is lonely because partners make decisions alone. Intimacy is difficult to achieve since partners do not develop ways of resolving anger and conflict in mutually satisfying ways.

Power-Based Decision Making

Some couples use power to win; they make decisions based on who can out-shout the other or on who is physically stronger than the other. They may draw children or friends or family into the fight or argument to side with them. They may also gain power by trying to weaken the other with insults or accusations aimed at the partner's weak spots. Power tactics destroy, not strengthen, a marriage. They are incompatible with the biblical principles of covenant marriage.

Default Decision Making

Some couples avoid making decisions; they let others or circumstances decide for them. Because they do not make choices, their relationship has no intentional direction or growth. Default decision making has no place in a covenant relationship that is intentional, in which each partner is to be responsible (see lesson 2).

Mutual Decision Making

Spouses are not to lord it over each other or use power to coerce each other. In a covenant marriage spouses should prayerfully make decisions together (see Matthew 18:19-20). Paul expected couples to reach decisions by mutual agreement (see 1 Corinthians 7:4-5a, NASB). Partners need to prayerfully consider the issue before them as they come to a decision both can agree on.

K. How were decisions primarily made in your family of origin?
❏ Autocratic
❏ Power-based
❏ Default
❏ Mutual

Rate the effectiveness of decision making in your family of origin.
❏ Seemed to work well
❏ Resulted in a lot of tension

> *Spouses are not to lord it over each other or use power to coerce each other*

How has the way decisions were made in your family of origin affected the way you and your mate make decisions? ❑ No effect ❑ Some effect ❑ Great effect

As you look back at the list of conflicts and problems you and your spouse have already successfully resolved in your relationship (exercise H), it is obvious that you already have skills in decision making. As is true with many couples, you may have used one or more of these ways at different times. However, you may have never given much thought to the ways you deal with conflict and to what patterns and skills work better for you than others. You need to celebrate and hold on to the things you do well as a couple. You may also want to change or strengthen aspects of your decision making.

L. Check the way you and your mate primarily make decisions.
   ❑ Autocratic
   ❑ Power-based
   ❑ Default
   ❑ Mutual

   Check how you feel about the way decisions are made.
   ❑ Basically satisfied
   ❑ Basically dissatisfied
   ❑ Need some degree of change

   How do you think your partner will respond to this same question?

> *"Love does not insist on its own way; it is not irritable or resentful; it does not rejoice at wrong, but rejoices in the right"*

SKILLS OF MUTUAL DECISION MAKING

Sharing Thoughts and Feelings
Lesson 7 focused on the skills of sharing thoughts and feelings: "I feel ... when you ... because. ..." Here are some reminders.
   Separate your observations, what you saw or heard, from your interpretations. For example:
   Observation—"When you and I disagree, we usually end up doing things my way."
   Thoughts and feelings—"I like to do things my way. I make good decisions. I feel secure and loved when you agree with me."
   Interpretations—"I wonder if you are afraid to say what you think."
   There is nothing magical in the formula "feelings, observations, interpretations" or "I feel... when you ... because ...," but it helps remind us that our perspective is relative and that our partner may have a different viewpoint. This approach helps us not to assume that our way is the right way but to look for the "right" beyond our own views: "Love does not insist on its own way; it is not irritable or resentful; it does not rejoice at wrong, but rejoices in the right" (1 Corinthians 13:5-6, RSV).

M. Rewrite the following paragraph to reflect the formula "I feel ... when you ... because. ..." How could it be said in light of 1 Corinthians 13:5b-6?

"Every time we go to Mother's, you head straight for the TV. Don't you know she's lonely? I might as well visit her by myself."

Listening to the Partner's View

Communicate with your eyes, your attention, and your words that you want to and are trying to understand. Turn off the TV. Put down the newspaper.

Encourage your partner to express his or her observations, feelings, and interpretations. As you listen, try to build a picture of how the situation looks and feels from your partner's perspective. Imagine that you are an actor playing your partner's part. Gather all the information you will need to do so. Ask questions like "Did I hear you say … ?" to check whether you are hearing and understanding. Do this until both you and your partner believe that you understand. Consider your spouse a partner in the joint task of understanding your relationship better and resolving conflict between you. Your partner should not be an opponent in a test of words or feelings.

These ideas may sound easy, but listening is quite difficult, especially if you and your spouse are in conflict.

- If I listen, I may find myself agreeing and will have to change my mind— a painful thing!
- If I listen, my partner may think I'm agreeing even if I do not.
- If I want to win the argument, I need to be thinking about what I am going to say next to defend my viewpoint, not about what my partner is saying to me.

Listening is difficult because we are usually more oriented to winning and convincing our partner that we are right than we are to understanding our partner and resolving the conflict in a way that will meet both of our needs and enhance our relationship. "A fool takes no pleasure in understanding, but only in expressing his opinion" (Proverbs 18:2, RSV).

Defining the Problem or Issue

If you have listened well and crawled behind your partner's eyes to see the issue from his or her perspective, the problem looks different now than it did before. A couple can define in many ways any issue it experiences. Each of you probably had a different problem definition to start with, and an outside observer could have added still another definition of the problem. There is no one way to define the problem. So the key is not finding the real problem as much as it is defining the problem in such a way that it can be resolved. Then both of you can have needs met as much as possible.

Answering the following questions helps define the problem in such a way that it can be resolved.

Is it a question of fact or a value difference? Questions of fact do not require conflict resolution; they require finding an expert source. For example, it does not make sense to argue about what is the last day of school, who spends the most time on housework, who spends more money on clothes, or how many holidays are in a year. Call the school, do a time study, add receipts, or consult a calendar!

As you listen, try to build a picture of how the situation looks and feels from your partner's perspective

112

If getting this information will not resolve the conflict, then the conflict is probably not what you thought it was, and you need a new definition. For example, it isn't who spends the most time on housework but that we both feel exhausted and pushed to do more than we can do. How can we get relief from our responsibilities?

Value differences, on the other hand, are the stuff of which conflict is made. Your "right" and your mate's "right" conflict with each other. You think children ought to do chores to earn their allowance; your mate thinks children ought to do chores as part of family living without having them tied to their allowance. Both of you can probably even find child-development experts who will substantiate the validity of your values.

What is the behavior we need to address? What behaviors are in conflict with each other; what do we say or do that creates problems for each other? If it is a decision we have to make, what choices face us in terms of what each of us will say or do?

Avoid defining problems as personality differences. For example, defining a housekeeping problem as "I think you're a slob, and you think I'm a pain in the neck" is probably not helpful. The only way to solve a problem defined in this way is to make basic personality changes—not an easy task! A better definition might be "I get angry when you leave your things on the kitchen cabinet, and you get frustrated because you don't have a place to put them out as you like to have them." The focus here is on behavior, not on personality traits, and behavior is much easier to change.

Do we have to agree about this, or can we live with our difference? The question about children's allowances requires agreement if spouses share their parenting responsibilities. Often, however, we may find ourselves quarreling about an issue that does not require our agreement. For example, it is fruitless for partners to argue about whether reading mysteries or reading newsmagazines is the best way to spend leisuretime. They can each read what they choose. If they find themselves arguing about it, however, there must be another issue besides reading material. Perhaps one partner wants to be able to discuss world affairs with the other. The other may want more playfulness in their relationship and thinks that the spouse's reading serious material keeps that from happening. The issue needs to shift from right reading material to the couple's desires for their relationship.

How strongly does each of us feel about this? Is this more important to one of us than the other? If so, perhaps one will be more willing to compromise, looking for solutions that will honor the other's strong values.

Trying Possible Solutions

Generate as many possible solutions to the problem as you can think of. Try to focus more on what you personally can do and less on what your partner can do. Contracts are often helpful ways to try solutions for a period of time. Then discuss the issue again to determine if both are satisfied or if the solution needs to be renegotiated.

N. Rewrite these statements so that a specific behavior change is called for.

Why is it that every night you are stepping into the shower when I'm getting into bed?

Try to focus more on what you personally can do and less on what your partner can do

_____

_____

Why do you always insist on driving and then ask me for directions?

_____

_____

I can't believe you're sitting here watching sports and I'm still cleaning up the kitchen.

_____

_____

Take time to review pages 24–26 about using contracts. (The development and use of contracts will be discussed further in lesson 10.)

CONFLICT IS PART OF COVENANT MARRIAGE

Part of mutual need meeting and intimacy in marriage is dealing with the conflicts between us and the decisions that face us. Often conflict is painful and creates anxiety. Yet when we are able to meet the challenges of conflict with resolution, our intimacy is deepened, and our commitment to each other is strengthened.

Conflict and anger are instruments of truth. The Bible is straightforward in condemning the practice of pretending that everything is all right instead of honestly facing the rifts in relationships. The prophets Jeremiah and Ezekiel both condemned prophets who said that all was well with Israel, ignoring the rift between the people and God: " 'They have healed the wound of my people lightly, saying, "Peace, peace," when there is no peace' " (Jeremiah 6:14; 8:11, RSV; also see Ezekiel 13:10-11,14-16.)

When something is wrong in a relationship, God pursues it and exposes it. Then the wrong can be healed and made right again. God wants the truth to come to light and engages in conflict in order to expose it.

Jesus often engaged in harsh conflict with the scribes and Pharisees and when He cleansed the temple (see Mark 11:15-19). In the same way, Christian partners need to take anger and conflict seriously in their relationship; we cannot ignore it or pretend that it does not exist.

O. **Identify your usual role when it comes to resolving conflicts in your marriage.**
   - ❏ **Instigator**—always having to take the lead
   - ❏ **Pacifist**—peace at all costs
   - ❏ **Peacemaker**—finding a workable solution
   - ❏ **The artful dodger**—adept at delaying tactics
   - ❏ **Golden-gloves champion**—ready to have at it

The biblical model of dealing with conflict ends with forgiveness. Even

When we are able to meet the challenges of conflict with resolution, our intimacy is deepened, and our commitment to each other is strengthened

though we have skills in listening and working through conflict, we are sinful creatures, and we find ourselves lapsing into saying spiteful words, hurting each other, and trying to win rather than trying to redeem the relationship. And our wounding words are often thrown back at us as we elicit in each other the mirror image of our defensiveness and self-centeredness. Our words do not return to us empty but unfortunately accomplish exactly our intentions—to hurt each other.

Forgiveness, then, often needs to be the last step in conflict resolution. Return to pages 34–36 and reread the material on forgiveness in light of the conflicts you and your spouse have experienced.

P. After a conflict has been resolved in your home, how do you relate to your partner? Check the statements that are true for you.
   ❏ I tend to hold a grudge.
   ❏ I can brush it aside rather quickly.
   ❏ It takes time for me to get over it completely.
   ❏ I need space to deal with my feelings.
   ❏ I move on to other things.
   ❏ I immediately want to be close again.
   ❏ I mull it over for a time afterward.
   ❏ I try to use the experience as a learning aid in dealing with similar situations in the future.

SUMMARY

Conflicts continue to occur throughout married life because of changes that require new ways of thinking and living. If only marriage partners could just agree to disagree. In most cases, however, a decision must be reached. The way partners make decisions may be as important as the decisions made.

Relationship factors may get in the way of good decision making. If we want to resolve a conflict in such a way that we win and feel superior, our partner is blamed for the problem, we get our partner's attention, we are martyred, or we don't have any part in making the decision, then we create problems that interfere with intimacy and communication.

Couples make decisions in four ways: autocratic (one person decides), power-based (one intimidates the other), default (no decision is made), and mutual (couples reach decisions by mutual agreement). Mutual decision making requires that partners share their thoughts and feelings clearly, listen intently, and define the problem in such a way that appropriate action can be taken. Although conflict is a part of covenant marriage, the biblical model of dealing with conflict ends in forgiveness.

CHECKPOINT

The following review exercise is designed to reveal whether you have achieved the learning goals for lesson 8. Answer each question. Correct answers are given after the final question.

Although conflict is a part of covenant marriage, the biblical model of dealing with conflict ends in forgiveness

1. Fill in the blanks to define *decision making:* Any _____ or conversation that results in a couple's _____what they will _____ or _____ in response to a _____ from within or without or to an _____ that creates _____ between them.

2. List the four ways couples make decisions and solve problems.
   a. _____
   b. _____
   c. _____
   d. _____

3. Which of the following is not a need that complicates decision making?
   ❑ a. superiority
   ❑ b. blaming
   ❑ c. refusing to decide

4. Draw a line from a specific action in column 1 to the skill involved in mutual decision making in column 2.

Column 1	Column 2
a. I feel … when you … because. …	x. Sharing thoughts and feelings
b. Communicate with your eyes, attention, and words.	y. Listening to the partner's views
c. Make a contract.	z. Defining the problem or issue
d. Build a picture of the way the situation looks from your partner's perspective.	
e. Specify the behavior that needs to change.	

5. Which of the actions listed above do you intend to use in making decisions during the coming week?

_____

Now check your answers.
1. activity, deciding, do, say, change, issue, conflict
2. a. autocratic, b. power-based, c. default, d. mutual
3. c
4. a. x, b. y, c. z, d. y, e. z
5. Personal response

LOOKING AHEAD

In our society we love hamburgers, our country, music, and other human beings. The word *love* is overused and abused. What does it mean to say that we love our mate?

In lesson 9 we will examine the various misconceptions of love and will identify biblical principles of love as commitment.

During the next 24 hours be aware of how many times and ways you use the word *love*.

UNIT 5

COMMITMENT TO A PARTNERSHIP OF LOVE

LOVE THAT LASTS A LIFETIME

Lesson 9

If love makes the world go around, our planet is rotating on a very shaky axle

LOOKING BACK

In lesson 8 we looked at five relationship issues that could keep a couple from developing skills in decision making. These issues would result in a win-lose situation rather than a win-win in which both partners have their needs met. Do you recall these five issues? If not, reread the summary of lesson 8.

We examined the four ways couples make decisions: autocratic, power-based, default, and mutual agreement. Mutual decision making was described as a means to help marriage partners work together to solve problems.

You were asked to identify the way you and your partner make decisions and to evaluate the effectiveness of your style. Have you made any changes during the past week as a result of your study? If so, perhaps you are finding that you share more freely, listen more intently, and forgive more easily.

The test of good decision making is to be able to clearly define the problem in such a way that appropriate action can be taken.

OVERVIEW

If love makes the world go around, our planet is rotating on a very shaky axle. Much of what passes for love in our culture has little to do with the kind of love experienced by covenant partners.

What distinguishes covenant, or active, love from other kinds of love? How does active love express itself daily? In this lesson we will examine 10 guidelines for expressing active love in specific situations in your married life.

When you complete this lesson, you will be able to—
* define *love* as commitment;
* compare and contrast love as commitment with various misconceptions of love;
* identify what the Bible says about love as commitment;
* list 10 principles of love as commitment that apply to marriage;
* evaluate the degree to which these principles are evident in your marriage relationship;
* implement at least one principle of love as commitment.

ACTIVE LOVE DEFINED

"Love and marriage, love and marriage, go together like a horse and carriage," goes the old song. Love is the horse and marriage the carriage that follows right behind. "You can't have one without the other," the song continues. This song expresses what many people in our culture expect of love and marriage: when you love someone, you marry that person; and married people love each other. When they stop loving each other, the marriage cannot last.

Love is a confusing word: I love pizza; I love old movies; I love that scarf on you; I love you. "I love you" can be offered as a rationale for sleeping together, as a reason for our eating at a Chinese restaurant because that is what you like instead of the Mexican restaurant I like, or as the sharing of deep feeling in an intimate moment.

Although they are quite different in many respects, all of these uses of *love* refer to love as a feeling. Dictionaries usually define *love* as intense affectionate feelings for another, strong fondness or enthusiasm for someone or something ("I love pizza"), or intense sexual desire for another. All of these feelings are considered difficult to control. Dictionary definitions are based on the current usage of a word in a particular culture. In summary, in our culture, love is an intense and almost uncontrollable feeling.

Covenant marriage is a partnership of love, but it is love defined not as our culture defines it. A biblical understanding of love is based not on feelings and emotions but on commitment and action. The Bible instructs us to love one another: " 'This is my commandment, that you love one another as I have loved you' " (John 15:12, RSV; also see 1 Corinthians 14:1a; Ephesians 5:1-2,25; 1 John 4:7,21).

A. Write several ways you know that Jesus loves you.

_____

_____

How many of the ways you listed are feelings? _____
How many are actions? _____

As any good parent knows, you cannot command someone else to feel certain feelings: "Now I want you two to love each other as a brother and sister ought to!" You can command someone else only to do certain things: "I want you to play together without calling each other names or hitting. I want you to share your toys."

Feelings cannot be commanded because we are not able to change them directly. We cannot make ourselves have certain feelings toward another person. We can, however, choose what we will do. Our behaviors may then have an effect on our feelings. The brother and sister who begin to share with each other may find that they begin to enjoy each other's company and perhaps even feel love for each other (see 1 John 3:18-20).

The only way to change feelings, then, is to change behavior—not to try to talk ourselves into a feeling of love but to act lovingly. For example, if I am afraid of a big dog coming toward me, telling myself not to be afraid is not going to change that knot in the pit of my stomach. The only way to change my feeling of fear is to do something—to run away or to reach out and pat the dog. Then my feelings may change from fear to either relief or pain. In the same way, when I am angry at my partner, I may not be able to make myself

> *A biblical understanding of love is based not on feelings and emotions but on commitment and action*

feel love. I can handle my anger and choose my behavior, however, and depending on what I choose to do, feelings of love may return.

Our love for each other in covenant marriage is based not on feelings, which often come and go, but on a commitment to act in loving ways. To distinguish the biblical understanding of love from the feeling-based love we hear advertised in popular love songs and movie romances, we can call it active love.

B. How is active love different from the love depicted by these song titles?
"Love Makes the World Go 'Round"
"I've Got That Lovin' Feeling"
"Love Me Tender"
"Baby Love"
"To All the Girls I've Loved Before"
"I'll Never Fall in Love Again"

_____

_____

Active love is a commitment freely chosen by partners

Active love is a commitment freely chosen by partners. Both in the initial commitment and in living in covenant with each other, our actions need to be based on the decision to be loving, not on our feelings. Anyone who has been married more than two weeks knows that at times we do not feel loving toward our partners. It is at that moment—when we no longer want to be together every moment of every day, when we would rather be somewhere else doing something else—that we can really begin to love each other actively.

Yet we live in the world; we cannot escape our culture's love affair with loving feelings that influences everything from what we brush our teeth with to the songs that echo in our cars, offices, kitchens, and minds. As we study our own marriages, then, we need to examine the influence of both biblical and cultural definitions of *love* in our own relationship. Listen to any love song on the radio, and it is clear that active love is not the love our culture loves!

C. Rate the type of love depicted in your favorite television shows or movies by placing dots on the following continuums.

fickle	steadfast
jealous	trusting
selfish	giving
short-term	long-term
conditional	unconditional

OTHER DEFINITIONS OF LOVE

Romantic Love

Romantic love is love American style. Romantic love is perhaps best captured in our phrase *falling in love*. The word *falling* is a good description of the helpless, out-of-control feeling associated with this kind of love. Romantic love is a passive experiencing of feelings, not an active choice of behavior. It implies that we really do not have any control of the "falling" ourselves, but we can make ourselves more attractive to increase our chances that someone else will fall in love with us or will continue to love us. We use a certain toothpaste to increase our sex appeal, or we read books or articles on how to please the opposite sex, or we wear a special perfume so that we might stay on his mind. We aim to make ourselves lovable, to put ourselves in an attractive package that will be desirable. We concentrate on being loved.

D. Describe the romantic aspects of your dating experience with your mate by answering these questions.

Where did you go that was for you a romantic spot?

_____

What particular words were used to convey romantic messages?

_____

What behaviors were romantic signals?

_____

Indicate the extent to which romance is still a part of your married life:
❏ Very important ❏ Somewhat important ❏ Needs a booster shot

Because romantic love is a state of being, there is also the illusion that it will last forever

Because romantic love is a state of being, there is also the illusion that it will last forever: "And the prince and princess got married and lived happily ever after." A man came to a counselor for help with some marital problems. He said to the counselor:

I don't want my wife to hear what I have to say, because I don't want to hurt her feelings. But I just don't have the same feelings I did when we married five years ago. The love is gone. I want to go away on a business trip and be like the commercial where the guy just can't wait to go and call his wife from his hotel room. Oh, I like to talk to my wife. But I don't feel that same desperate sense of wanting to be with her all the time. And my heart doesn't race anymore when I see her. The love is gone.

For him, the enchantment of romantic love had faded. He seemed to think he was not even responsible for no longer loving his wife. If we can't help falling into something, how can we help falling out of it?

If love is based solely on feelings, that love is bound to wax and wane with the tides of intimacy, sexual fulfillment, anger, and conflict in marriage. Covenant marriage, on the other hand, is based on commitment and responsibility of the partners to each other, not on a helpless response to feelings.

That does not mean that covenant marriage and romantic, passionate love are incompatible. Many couples marry because of the romantic, passionate love they have for each other, and it may continue throughout their relationship. Romance and passion may spice up the lives of covenant partners; however, they are not the meat and potatoes of their relationship with each other. The focus of covenant partners is on *acting* lovingly toward each other, not *being* in love.

> *Romance and passion may spice up the lives of covenant partners; however, they are not the meat and potatoes of their relationship with each other*

E. **What are some little acts of love you could perform that would express TLC (tender, loving care) to your partner this week? Here are some suggestions: bring her a cup of coffee, offer to rub his shoulders, whisper something sweet in her ear, leave him a note where he will find it. Now you name some.**

_____

_____

Infatuation

Infatuation is an adolescent version of romantic love. The focus is often a popular entertainer or perhaps even a peer (the captain of the football team or the head cheerleader) who is worshiped from afar. Infatuation is lovesickness; the infatuated person has difficulty eating, sleeping, or working for thinking of the other.

F. **What are some of the myths about your mate that early infatuation may have built in your mind? Has the destruction of these myths strengthened or weakened your love? Why?**

_____

_____

Infatuation is basically self-centered; we are tied up in our own feelings and may know very little about the other person except that she is the most beautiful woman in the world, he has a voice that even the angels stop singing to hear, and we melt when we see him or her. Only a superficial relationship exists, if any relationship at all. Knowledge about the other tends to shatter the infatuation, which is based on an ideal we have built in our minds instead of the real, living, breathing person. As a relationship develops between persons, the infatuation may end or develop into a loving relationship.

G. **What is the danger of a married person's allowing himself or herself to become infatuated with an unapproachable "star" of the opposite sex (TV personality, sports hero, etc.)?**

_____

_____

Sexual Attraction or Lust

Sexual arousal has been confused in our society with the feelings of falling in love. Sexual impulses, however, often have little to do with love. We can be aroused sexually even by someone we dislike in other ways and with whom we certainly would not want to establish a lifetime covenant.

When we let our feelings control us, when we choose to let our sexual attraction to another dominate our thoughts about that other person, the result is lust. The other becomes simply an object for our pleasure, not a person who is a unique creation of God to be cherished and respected.

Sexual attraction is a significant aspect of covenant marriage. We use our feelings of attraction to build an intimate and loving relationship. Mature sexual love does not focus only on the spouse's sexuality but on his or her total personhood. Instead of seeking self and self's needs, covenant-marriage partners seek a deeper relationship with each other.

H. Married sexual love needs to be nourished like a tender plant. Two tired persons at the end of an exhausting day find it difficult to establish a proper climate for sexual intimacy. What can you do this week to—

vary the time (and place?) of your sexual expression?

_____

enhance your sexual attractiveness?

_____

make sex an enjoyable experience for your mate?

_____

Altruistic Love

Altruistic love is closest to what we have called the active love of covenant marriage. The Greek word *agape* describes God's love for people and the kind of love people are capable of when the Holy Spirit works in their lives. In *agape* love, the focus is caring for the other, not meeting my own needs; it is selfless love. *Agape* love is self-giving, other-centered, and committed to the personhood of the loved one. It is modeled after the love Jesus had for His followers. Refer to our earlier discussion of active love to place this in perspective.

Friendship Love

Happily married couples, when asked about their feelings for each other, often comment that they are not only lovers but also best friends. They enjoy each other's company; they choose to share time, activities, and themselves with each other.

Friendship love and altruistic love are important ingredients in the active love of a covenant marriage. But active love does not exclude some of the other kinds of love; certainly there are elements of sexual attraction and romance in our relationship, or we probably never would have married in the first place. Paul makes it clear that sexual expression is a key component of marriage between Christians (see 1 Corinthians 7:2-5).

Agape *love is self-giving, other-centered, and committed to the personhood of the loved one*

123

I. List one way active love is like or unlike each of the following.

Romantic love: _____

Infatuation: _____

Lust: _____

Altruistic love: _____

Friendship: _____

*Take control of
your own behavior
and choose what
you will do*

PRINCIPLES OF LOVE AS COMMITMENT

Active love focuses on what we do that is loving, not on how we feel. Romantic love is something you passively wait to feel; active love is something you can create. We can state some guidelines, then, for developing an actively loving relationship between covenant partners.

Act in loving ways, whether or not you feel loving. Take control of your own behavior and choose what you will do. Jesus said to turn the other cheek and walk the extra mile even for the enemy. He did not expect that we would feel like doing these things. But His disciples were to act in these ways, even though they might feel like striking back or throwing down the Roman soldier's things in the dusty road.

As disciples of Christ, we are to choose not to return injury for injury, insult for insult. When our spouse blames us for a bad day at work, our impulse is to hurl back: "How could it be my fault? You need to start taking responsibility for yourself and stop using me as an excuse for everything that goes wrong!"

Instead, active love uses skills of listening, sifting through and trying to understand what the partner is thinking and feeling. Anger is put in language that the spouse can hear, not language that simply vents our frustration at being blamed. You may want to think together about a way to respond lovingly to such an accusation and the feelings that such a response would create in you and also in your partner.

To act in love does not mean sugary sweetness, ignoring the anger and conflict that develop. In fact, it means just the opposite. Acting in love means attacking the issues that separate us and resolving conflicts that are a seedbed for anger.

J. Richard has just come home from work. He skipped lunch, sat in a traffic jam, and brought home a briefcase full of work. When he comes through the kitchen door, he sees that dinner is still cooking; his two sons are playing a loud, active game of chase; and their large, sleeping German Shepherd is blocking his doorway to the bedroom. Describe ways Richard might respond to this situation that would reflect his own mood and feelings.

_____

_____

Describe ways Richard could respond that would reflect active love for his family, even when he doesn't feel like it.

_____

_____

Describe ways Richard's wife might respond both positively and negatively in light of Richard's mood.

_____

_____

Affirm that your love for each other is a life commitment. We belong to each other, for better or worse, for richer or poorer, in sickness and in health. "Love never ends" (1 Corinthians 13:8, RSV). Yet in the heat of an argument, it is too easy to drop the big bomb: "If you don't . . . then you can just see what it'll be like around here without me." Often such a threat means "I have had all I can take. This is serious; you had better sit up and take notice." Because it is the ultimate threat, it often ends the argument. There may be no resolution, or the partner may angrily and wordlessly give in. Because it has such a powerful effect, it is quite tempting to use threats again, even though such threats devastate the partners' trust and the relationship's intimacy.

K. Check any of these threats you may have used "in the heat of battle" with your partner.
   ❑ I'll go home to Mama.
   ❑ I won't love you anymore.
   ❑ I won't be here when you get back.
   ❑ I've helped you out for the last time.
   ❑ I'll take away your checkbook.
   ❑ I'll take the kids, and you'll never see them again.
   ❑ Other: _____

Withdrawing or threats of withdrawing love or companionship should be banned as a conflict strategy in covenant marriage. They are usually used to manipulate each other and do not represent the serious thinking that needs to be involved if ending the marriage is really being considered. Partners need to trust each other, and it is difficult to trust someone who is threatening destruction.

Show empathy for each other. To show empathy means to communicate to the partner that you understand what he or she is feeling and thinking and what is important to the partner. Such empathy powerfully communicates our love to each other. Empathy requires commitment, skills of listening, and knowing ourselves.

1. Empathy requires choice, the will to understand, a decision. We must commit ourselves to the partner and make the decision to move beyond ourselves into the experience of the other. As discussed in lesson 7, one of the most difficult times to make that choice is when we are in conflict with each other. It is far easier to defend our position than to make the conscious choice to put self in the place of the other person and see how the situation looks from the partner's perspective.

2. Empathy requires skill. We can want to understand the other person a great

To show empathy means to communicate to the partner that you understand what he or she is feeling and thinking and what is important to the partner

125

deal and not be able to if we have not developed the skills of listening, as discussed in lesson 8. The love of covenant partners reflects God's love for us. God knows us inside out: the secrets of our hearts (see Psalm 44:21) and the thoughts of our minds (see Psalm 94:11; also see Luke 11:17), the deeds we have done (see Psalm. 69:5), and our words even before we speak them (see Psalm 139:4). God knows our sufferings (see Exodus 3:7). In the same way, we are to love each other enough to know each other. One way we can get this kind of knowledge of each other is to learn effective skills of listening. We can never know our partners as completely as God knows us. However, that does not mean we cannot work to develop our abilities of understanding. Most partners feel deeply loved and respected when we attempt to understand, even if our attempts at times fall far short.

3. Empathy requires knowing ourselves. What are our biases, our values, and the limits of our understanding? Only by knowing ourselves in this way can we be aware of our blind spots in understanding our partners, of the distortions that are likely in our pictures of our spouse's thoughts and feelings. We need to know whether our perception is distorted by a log in our own eye before we try to see, much less try to do something about, a speck in the eye of our partner (see Matthew 7:3-5).

L. **Check the following distortions that often affect the way you hear and perceive your mate.**
   ❑ **Comparing your mate to her/his mother or father**
   ❑ **Comparing your mate to your mother or father**
   ❑ **Letting work pressures get to you**
   ❑ **Letting the children get to you**
   ❑ **Irritability or moodiness**
   ❑ **Selfishness, self-centeredness**
   ❑ **Unrealistic expectations**

Share yourself deeply and broadly. Active love shares the deepest part of ourselves, trusting the other with our secret longings and thoughts we share with no one else. Active love also shares broadly—in the many areas and aspects of our lives, including our work, our recreation, our religious lives, our sexual selves, our serious selves, and our playful selves.

Empathy without sharing is not active love; instead, it comes across as cross examination or trying to counsel our partners. Our partners may feel as though they are expected to share themselves; yet they are not privy to our own thoughts, feelings, and dreams.

M. **What is something you would like to be able to share with your mate about—**

a dream (goal)? _____

an idea? _____

a secret? _____

a problem? _____

Active love shares the deepest part of ourselves, trusting the other with our secret longings and thoughts we share with no one else

126

Will you trust your mate enough to share with her or him this week?
❏ Yes ❏ No

Share your resources deeply and broadly. Covenant partners share their resources with each other—extra time to listen, a special talent that helps the partner with a seemingly impossible task, a bite of our dessert, a corner of the apartment to spread out a project.

There are other less tangible resources we share. Compliments and constructive criticism mean much more coming from a spouse who knows us inside and out than from a stranger who may not understand the context of our behavior. Our judgment is a precious resource to be used wisely, not to be dumped on each other. For example, a wife may ask her husband his reaction to a speech she has prepared or to the way she handled the children at a stressful time. A husband may ask a wife for her opinion in clothes that suit him or the way he responded to an angry neighbor.

The key in using our judgment as a resource is to allow the partner to ask for it or, if we must offer it, check first whether it is something they really want from us before we blurt it out. Coal is a wonderfully valuable resource in a January snowstorm for a family in Rochester, Minnesota. The same pile of coal dumped in the front yard of a family in Miami, Florida, however, is not a resource; it is a dirty mess. Be sure your partner is cold and has a furnace that can use them before you heap your coals of wisdom on him or her.

N. Which of these does your mate most often hear from you?
    ❏ Compliments ❏ Criticism ❏ Constructive criticism

Write one or more compliments you intend to pay your partner this week.

_____

_____

Love with self-discipline and responsibility. A loving partner exercises self-discipline and responsibility. We are always "in training" as lovers; we practice listening, sharing ourselves, being there when our partner needs us, and following through on what we say we will do.

Some of the highest experiences in married life come as a result of acting responsibly with each other. For example, many couples in recent years have experienced the birth of a child as a time when the husband stood by and responded to the needs of the wife, coaching and encouraging through the difficult hours of labor despite his own fatigue, worry, and hunger. And many other times we stand by each other, sometimes when it is painful and difficult.

O. Describe a time in your married life when you were there for each other, when both of you acted responsibly and with sensitivity on a significant occasion.

_____

_____

_____

Likewise, some of the greatest marital distress comes when partners act irresponsibly and undependably. Nothing can set off anger in my partner quite

Some of the highest experiences in married life come as a result of acting responsibly with each other

like my not doing what I say I will do. Infidelity creates a rift in marriage because it often destroys the basic trust partners have in each other to live up to the commitment each has made.

Treat your partner with respect. Our partners have different ideas, feelings, thoughts, and dreams than we have. We can work hard to understand each other, but all the empathy in the world will not melt the differences. Respect means acknowledging our differences and recognizing that despite our covenant with each other, we will remain individuals, separate and distinct from each other. We were not created alike and should not try to re-create each other in our own likeness.

Recognize that active love is a part of Christian discipleship training. Our acts of piety and worship are worthless if we do not faithfully love our covenant partners (see Malachi 2:13-14). What we do to our mates, we also do to the Lord (see Ephesians 5:22; Matthew 25:31-46).

Practice forgiveness with each other. Active love must always include the practice of forgiveness. You will want to review the material on forgiveness in lesson 2.

Depend on God, not your own efforts, for active loving. Taken together, the other nine guidelines for active love seem impossible. We can accomplish nothing except by God's grace. Without God our self-centeredness overcomes us; our hearts condemn us (see 1 John 3:20). God is bigger than we are and can enable us when our will and determination are weak and our hearts fail us. God is indeed a rock and a fortress and a sure defender. Marriages built on God's promises and faithfulness are stronger than those built on human loyalty. Covenant marriage requires our commitment to the work and discipline of loving, but our work is always in the context of God's grace and hand working through us.

P. Reread each of the 10 guideline statements, beginning on page 124. Check those you feel describe you to some degree. Write X beside those you want to work on in the coming weeks.

Marriages built on God's promises and faithfulness are stronger than those built on human loyalty

SUMMARY

Covenant love differs from the popular, cultural usage of the word *love* by commitment and actions. Covenant partners act lovingly toward each other, whether or not they feel like it.

Unlike romantic love, which is based on feelings, or infatuation, which is based on a superficial ideal, covenant love is other-centered and self-giving. Lust uses the desired object for its own pleasure; active love is committed to the other's total personhood.

Ten principles were given for expressing active love in daily situations. These principles are:
1. Act in loving ways, whether or not you feel loving.
2. Affirm that your love for each other is a life commitment.
3. Show empathy for each other.
4. Share yourself deeply and broadly.
5. Share your resources deeply and broadly.
6. Love with self-discipline and responsibility.
7. Treat your partner with respect.
8. Recognize that active love is a part of Christian discipleship training.

128

9. Practice forgiveness with each other.
10. Depend on God, not your own efforts, for active loving.

CHECKPOINT

The following review exercise is designed to reveal whether you have achieved the learning goals for lesson 9. Answer each question. Correct answers are given after the final question.

1. The one word that best describes active love is—
   - ❑ a. commitment;
   - ❑ b. patience;
   - ❑ c. endurance;
   - ❑ d. responsibility.

2. Match these misconceptions of love with the descriptive statements on the right.
   - ___ a. romance   x. based on selfish needs
   - ___ b. infatuation   y. based on an ideal
   - ___ c. lust   z. based on feelings

3. Which of the following is not one of the first four principles of active love?
   - ❑ a. I act lovingly when I feel like it.
   - ❑ b. I am committed to my mate for life.
   - ❑ c. I show empathy for my mate.
   - ❑ d. I share myself deeply and broadly.

4. Fill in the blanks to complete the last six principles of active love.
   - a. I _____ my _____ deeply and broadly.
   - b. I love with _____ and

     _____.
   - c. I _____ my partner with _____.
   - d. I recognize that _____ _____ is a part of

     _____ _____

     _____.
   - e. I _____ _____ my mate.
   - f. I depend on _____, not my own _____,
      for active loving.

5. Write the one guideline you most want to work on during the coming week.

   _____

   _____

Now check your answers.
1. a
2. a. z, b. y, c. x
3. a
4. a. share, resources; b. self-discipline, responsibility; c. treat, respect; d. active love, Christian discipleship training; e. practice forgiving; f. God, efforts
5. Personal response

One of the most popular features on cameras is the automatic focus. Pictures do not come out blurred. It would be nice if our marriages could have an automatic-focus button. We could keep our marital picture in balance and harmony, with the proper perspective on our blessings and problems.

We will have the opportunity to focus on goals for the future development of our marriages as covenant relationships when we study and experience lesson 10, "Focusing on the Future."

FOCUSING ON THE FUTURE

Lesson 10

Lesson 9 centered on the kind of love that will last a lifetime. Active love is modeled after the kind of love Jesus had for His followers. This *agape* love is self-giving, other-centered, and committed to the loved one's personhood.

All of us have difficulty expressing that kind of love on a day-to-day basis. Ten guidelines were given to help you apply the principles of active love. How many of them can you recall? If you can remember five or fewer, look back at the summary of lesson 9 for a quick review.

Which guidelines did you decide to work on during the week? What actions on your part have demonstrated your willingness to change behavior patterns or to develop new ways of relating?

OVERVIEW

Do you ever wish for a crystal ball that would reveal the future? Psychologists and sociologists tell us that we can literally change the course of the future by the simple act of goal setting. By determining where we want to be and what we want to be doing 1 year, 2 years, or even 25 years from now, we establish habits, skills, and knowledge that will eventually get us where we want to be.

A covenant marriage does not just happen. A covenant marriage must be planned. Patterns of relating, lifestyles, and personal habits must be molded into a strategy for attaining a partnership of love.

This lesson will encourage you to dream great dreams about what marriage can and should be for you. You will also develop the goals and objectives that will bring those dreams to reality.

When you complete this lesson, you will be able to—
* define *covenant marriage* as a partnership of love;
* evaluate the covenant you and your mate wrote in the early sessions of this course;
* assess with your mate your understanding of your marriage as covenant;
* set short- and long-term goals for the future development of your marriage as a covenant relationship;
* select and begin to implement one of your goals.

RESPONDING TO CRISES

Many things happen to us in life that we do not choose: illness, death of a

We can literally change the course of the future by the simple act of goal setting

family member, unemployment, who our neighbors are, new opportunities, our partner's moods and feelings, our own feelings and needs, mid-life crises. But we can choose how to respond to life events. Research on family crisis and stress indicates that it is not so much the stress or crisis itself but how couples choose to respond to what happens that determines the outcome for their relationship. One couple can experience a crisis such as the loss of a job or having a chronically ill parent move in with them and flounder as they are overcome by stress. Another couple may end up feeling closer to each other and strengthened as a result of facing the same crisis.

A. Read the following case study and answer the questions that follow: Montie and Marie had a series of unexpected financial drains on their budget the week before they had planned to take a second honeymoon.

Describe ways Montie and Marie could react to this situation that would put a strain on their relationship.

_____

_____

Describe how Montie and Marie might respond to this stress that would have positive effects on their relationship.

_____

_____

It is not so much the stress or crisis itself but how couples choose to respond to what happens that determines the outcome for their relationship

A number of factors make the difference between coming through crisis stronger than before and being overcome by crisis. These factors characterize ways couples can choose to relate to each other; they are not just luck.

A couple understands and accepts that they are in a stressful situation. They do not pretend that everything is normal but extend grace to each other, knowing that each may be moodier, more forgetful, and less able to perform normal tasks as well.

A couple locates the problem in their relationship instead of in a particular individual. "We are in this together" is the theme, not "I hope you can handle your problem." The crisis that descends on one is shared by both; when the wife loses her job, they both discuss and explore alternatives.

A couple looks for solutions to the problem or crisis rather than who is to blame. "What can we do? What are our options?" sets the discussion tone, not "This would have never happened if you hadn't ..." or "I was afraid this would happen, but you just didn't listen to me."

Partners communicate clearly and directly their commitment to and affection for each other. Sometimes holding each other and the words "I love you" are needed medicine.

Partners talk about the problem or crisis over and over. If one is facing cancer surgery, they talk together about their fears, the possibilities, their hopes, and their prayers. They do not pretend everything is normal and avoid the topic in hopes of not upsetting each other.

Partners are close to each other. Even couples who often interact more in an individuality style than in a unity style find themselves doing more together, sharing in each other's activities that they normally do separately, spending more time talking. They do not try to avoid the problem or crisis by avoiding each other.

Partners' roles are flexible and shifting. During a crisis each pitches in wherever needed, regardless of whose job is whose. Adding a new baby is a crisis event because of the change it creates in the family. During the time of adjustment, the roles of cook, housecleaner, and parent-in-the-night may shift back and forth, depending on the fatigue and responsibilities elsewhere that each is carrying.

Couples search for and use outside resources. Partners find others who have faced similar crises and learn from their experiences. They may use resources such as a neighborhood teenager to help with chores and fast food to help with meals. They may negotiate some exchanges: "I would be happy to check on your mother every day while you and your wife are on vacation, and maybe you could do the same for my mother while we are away." They read everything they can read about the problem or crisis they are facing to find resources and helpful ideas.

Partners learn to deal with their feelings and needs in constructive ways. Because they both are experiencing the tension of added stress, anger is a greater possibility than at other times. Spouses need to be careful that they neither hurt each other ventilating their feelings nor withdraw from each other. During periods of crisis, it is important to make sure that drugs and alcohol do not become an easy escape from facing the crisis together.[1]

B. Identify a recent crisis or problem you and your partner faced. Go back through the list of factors presented above and place a check beside those that describe the way you and your partner coped with the situation. Write X beside the factors that caused you difficulty.

As you looked at the characteristics of a healthy response to crisis, perhaps you noticed that each one reflects a choice by the partners. There is the choice, for example, to face the problem or crisis together instead of trying to put it on the back of the other partner, the choice of talking about the problem instead of trying to avoid it. Making choices is the key to a healthy, growing marriage. Choices can be made in response to problems and crises; we also make choices in response to opportunities.

C. Look back at the factors beside which you wrote X in the preceding exercise. List one or more choices by you or your partner that made the situation more difficult.

_____

_____

What better choice(s) might have improved the situation?

_____

_____

Making choices is the key to a healthy, growing marriage

133

This lesson is also a time for you and your partner to make choices. You have been exposed to nine lessons about covenant marriage. What will you do with what you have learned? How has this experience changed your life together? How do you want it to change your life? This can be a time of reflection and planing. Below are listed the major topics that have been discussed in the previous nine lessons.

Remember as you discuss these together as a couple to let your interaction with each other reflect the principles of a healthy response to crisis as presented earlier in this lesson. Any change or possibility for change in a marriage presents a crisis, even if it is a "happy" crisis. It is a point of decision, perhaps of changing directions.

CONCEPTS OF COVENANT MARRIAGE—A REVIEW

D. Place a check beside each concept you feel you understand and have tried to incorporate into your marriage. Write X beside the concept if you do not remember the content of a topic or if it raises questions for you. The page numbers are listed so that you can return to an earlier lesson for a brief review. Draw a star beside each concept that represents a skill you need to work on.

Marriage as Covenant
❑ A covenant is not the wedding-day vows but the fruit of a loving, faithful relationship between a man and a woman (p. 18).
❑ Covenant partners take responsibility for their own actions, not blame their partners for the results of what they do (p. 19).
❑ Covenant partners respect each other's freedom and do not try to force the other to behave, think, or feel certain ways (p. 20).
❑ Covenants are rooted in actions, not feelings (p. 21).
❑ Covenant partners nurture their relationship, not drain it (p. 23).
❑ Covenant partners freely offer steadfast loyalty and don't keep score (p. 23).

Marriage as Promise
Covenant marriage—
❑ is permanent (p. 29);
❑ costs (p. 30);
❑ is both freedom and obligation (p. 30);
❑ is defined by the partners, not by others' expectations (p. 32);
❑ is intentional (p. 33);
❑ promises unconditional love (p. 34);
❑ promises forgiveness (p. 34);
❑ promises comfort (p. 36);
❑ promises hope (p. 37).

Honoring Our Uniqueness
❑ We do not take personally every action and word of our partner (p. 44).
❑ We do not retreat from the rest of the world (p. 45).
❑ Covenant partners are individuals, not just halves of a couple (p. 47).
❑ Individuality brings the possibility of change (p. 48).
❑ Individuality requires trust (p. 48).

Any change or possibility for change in a marriage presents a crisis, even if it is a "happy" crisis

❑ Unity builds intimacy (p. 48).
❑ Unity requires the ability to resolve differences (p. 48).

Celebrating Our Unity
❑ Because we are made in God's image, we have authority over and responsibility for creation (p. 54).
❑ Because we are made in God's image, our relationships are to be characterized by love, not power (p. 55).
❑ We are unique as a couple (p. 57).
❑ Our differences make harmony and cooperation possible (p. 60).
❑ Our differences require compromise (p. 60).
❑ Our similarities are the basis for friendship and intimacy (p. 61).
❑ Our similarities require balance (p. 61).

Called to Purpose
Marriages have many purposes, both in the beginning and as partners continue in covenant with each other. These purposes include the following.
❑ Providing protection (p. 69)
❑ Coping with social pressure (p. 69)
❑ Providing status (p. 70)
❑ Meeting economic needs (p. 70)
❑ Developing intimacy—sexual fulfillment and friendship (pp. 71–72)
❑ Accomplishing common, shared goals (p. 73)

Called to Partnership
Areas in which we may share a common commitment and calling:
❑ Parenting (p. 80)
❑ Careers (p. 82)
❑ Homemaking (p. 84)
❑ Church and community (p. 85)
❑ The world (p. 85)

Managing Anger and Conflict
Two strategies damage relationships:
❑ Ventilating (p. 95)
❑ Withdrawing (p. 96)
Three strategies strengthen relationships:
❑ Postponing (p. 97)
❑ Reinterpreting (p. 98)
❑ Facing the issue (p. 99)

Making Decisions and Resolving Conflict
Four skills for mutual decision making:
❑ Sharing thoughts and feelings (p. 111)
❑ Listening to the partner's view (p. 112)
❑ Defining the problem or issue (p. 112)
❑ Trying possible solutions (p. 113)

Love That Lasts a Lifetime
Principles of love as commitment:

How has this experience changed your life together?

135

❑ Act in loving ways, whether or not you feel loving (p. 124).
❑ Affirm that your love for each other is a life commitment (p. 125).
❑ Show empathy for each other (p. 125).
❑ Share yourself deeply and broadly (p. 126).
❑ Share your resources deeply and broadly (p. 127).
❑ Love with self-discipline and responsibility (p. 127).
❑ Treat your partner with respect (p. 128).
❑ Recognize that active love is a part of Christian discipleship training (p. 128).
❑ Practice forgiveness with each other (p. 128).
❑ Depend on God, not your own efforts, for active loving (p. 128).

E. Take out the covenant you and your partner wrote in group session 1. Look back over this summary section. Which of these points did you include in your covenant? Which would you like to add to your covenant? List the changes or additions here.

_____

_____

Goals spell out what kinds of changes we intend to make to help our covenants become reality

A NEW COVENANT

As you reviewed the major points of this course and looked at your written covenant, you realized that many of these points are part of the covenant you have with each other, even though when you wrote your covenant in group session 1, you did not include them all. You may also have identified characteristics of covenant relationships that you want to be a part of your covenant with each other that will require changes in your relationship. Remember that covenants are not contracts, not time-limited, but they are promises and commitments you make to another. The following, for example, might be a marital covenant.

We covenant to act lovingly and faithfully toward each other. We will each take responsibility for what we do and will not blame each other for our decisions. We will love each other even when we do not feel like it.

F. Write on a separate sheet of paper a draft of a new covenant that represents the changes you would like to make in your original version. Be prepared to share your revision with your partner during the group session.

MARRIAGE GOALS

Covenants are timeless; they say what we commit ourselves to but not how we will bring it to pass. They state our ideals. Goals spell out what kinds of changes we intend to make to help our covenants become reality. They are the general directions we commit ourselves to in order to achieve our covenant promises. Goals reflect what we want to happen in the future. Through God's leadership, couples can develop goals that help their covenant become reality. Some goals that fit the covenant above, for example, might be:

1. To learn to share our feelings and perceptions with each other instead of blame each other.
2. To develop a shared ministry together as one aspect of our love in action by

volunteering to be foster grandparents for a single teenage parent.

3. To develop more similarity by doing some of the same chores instead of dividing them as rigidly as we have in the past.

Goals give a clearer picture of what we will work on together than the general promises of our covenant. They identify key pieces of our covenant with each other that we think need special attention and define some ways we might fulfill our covenant promises.

G. Write one, two, or three goal statements below that represent short-term and long-range plans for your married life.

1. _____

2. _____

3. _____

OBJECTIVES

Objectives are the assembly instructions for our goals. If we glue tab C to tab A and insert the mainspring, we should come up with whatever we set out to make. Of course, there is no real guarantee that if we follow the instructions, our gadget will come out exactly as we thought it would. Objectives are the same way; they are our best effort, with God's leadership, to put our goals into everyday actions that should, if we work at them, accomplish our goals.

Two problems may arise. First, we may develop excellent objectives but not follow up on them. If that happens, we can hardly expect to achieve our goals.

Second, we may develop excellent objectives and achieve them, but they may not accomplish our goals as we had hoped they would. For example, Marla and Tom wanted to improve their communication. The objective they hoped would achieve that goal included using the listening skills described in lesson 8. They became skillful at listening to each other, however, and were still not satisfied with their communication. As they talked together about the reasons they were dissatisfied, they realized they also needed to learn to share their thoughts, feelings, and dreams with each other and to take responsibility for themselves rather than blame each other. A single objective about listening was not enough to reach their goal of satisfying communication.

Even though it is possible that our objectives will not always lead us to our goals, we must have objectives. To try to achieve goals without objectives because they may not always help us toward our goals is like taking a trip to a new place without a map for fear we might misread it at some point. Yet what chance do we have of reaching this new place without a map? Marla and Tom would not have realized their need to work on sharing with each other if they had not committed themselves to their objective about listening.

H. Two of the following statements are objectives that lead to the accomplishment of the third statement, which is a goal. Label the goal statement G and the two objective statements O.
___ Join our neighborhood baby-sitting co-op.
___ Spend more time together doing the things we enjoy.
___ Take off work every other Thursday afternoon.

Objectives are the assembly instructions for our goals

To develop an objective, take a goal and think about what it would look like if you could see it. The objective is simply the painting of your vision. Here are the pieces that need to be included in an objective.

Who is supposed to do or say what? What will you and your partner be doing if you accomplish your objective? Be as specific as possible. What will you say? What actions will you take? Who will be doing what, not what attitudes or feeling will you have (that no one—including you—can see)? Imagine that you are coaching actors in a play. Tell them what the camera and the audio recorder need to record.

- Sharon will call the foster-grandparent program. We will plan together to visit our assigned family and talk with the mother about what we can do.
- We will tell each other our feelings and perceptions in conflict situations. When one hears the other sharing feelings and perceptions, the hearer will write two points on the sheet on the refrigerator. We will subtract a point if either says, "It's your fault because …" or "If you hadn't … then."

When stating who is to say or do what, be positive, not negative. You cannot see something *not* happen, only something happening in its place. "We will not blame each other" is a negative statement. The statement can be turned into a positive statement by focusing on what we will do in place of the undesirable behavior: "We will share our feelings and perceptions."

How much, how often, when? This is especially important for the kinds of objectives that spell out roles and responsibilities. "Susan will wash the cars *once each week*." "John will do the dishes *anytime before* 9:00." In our examples:

- Sharon will call before the end of next week.
- Anytime one or both of us are angry or we are in conflict.

Set yourself up to win. Make the objective small enough that you can obtain it. You can always revise it and make change happen faster, but it is hard to pick up and start again after you have failed at an overly ambitious objective. For example, if the goal is for the husband and wife to learn to do each other's household tasks, then it is more reasonable to begin with "Jack will fix dinner once a week" if Jack has never cooked before than to say "Jack will take over all meal preparation."

The objective regarding the foster-grandparent program marks a new dimension to Sharon and Jim's relationship. But their objectives called simply for a phone call and an initial visit. The objective did not set them up for possible failure by suggesting that they and a teenage single parent become as close as family to one another in a three-week period.

When/how will you evaluate? Objectives are time-limited. They need to have an ending time or at least a time to evaluate whether to transform the objective into an ongoing part of life together. For example:

- We will add up points at the end of the week and decide whether we want to continue giving each other points for stating feelings and perceptions.

Jim and Sharon saw by the total number of points they earned, as well as the number they had to subtract, how well they did. If they decided to continue their objective, they could compare from week to week. They certainly did not want their sharing always to be tied to points recorded on the refrigerator. But their objective gave them a boost into a new behavior pattern they could later decide to continue without having to prompt themselves with points.

I. Read the following objective. Circle the part that tells who. Underline what

To develop an objective, take a goal and think about what it would look like if you could see it will be done. Put a wavy line under how much, how often, or when. Bracket the part that gives the evaluation period.

> During the week of August 10–17 Nancy and Mark will both get out of bed every morning when the alarm goes off the first time. On August 18 they will total the number of times they accomplished their objective.

J. Write objectives that will lead to accomplishing one of the goals you wrote in exercise G. Remember to follow the guidelines for writing objectives.

_____

_____

_____

CONTRACTS

Contracts are a special kind of objective that always involve both partners and spell out what the outcome will be for reaching the objective. For example, when Jim and Sharon collected 15 points between them, they had a special dinner out. They both were involved in the behavior, and they both were involved in the reward.

Objectives need to focus on positive behaviors, what you want to happen, not what you don't want to happen. In the same way, contracts need to focus on rewarding the change you want to happen, not on punishing failure. Notice that Jim and Sharon's contract contained no punishment. Blaming slows down accumulating points, but there was no penalty, such as having to wash dishes for a week.

You will want to review pages 24–26 about contracts. Briefly, contracts—
- are for positive change;
- involve specific actions;
- include both partners offering something new and positive;
- are time-limited, not permanent.

Contracts may focus on one partner's individual behavior, such as a change the partner wants to work on. However, both partners' behavior needs to be involved in some way if it is a relationship contract. For example, Jim wanted to work on taking responsibility for his own behavior in conflict situations instead of blaming Sharon. They formed a contract in which, every time Sharon knew Jim was upset but said something like "I know I am responsible for this because ..." or "Let's see how we can deal with this," she told him how much she appreciated him. Each freely offered something to the other. Jim offered a share of the responsibility for their partnership, and Sharon offered her spoken appreciation and willingness to work with him. Even though the focus was initially on Jim's behavior, the task defined by the objective was a joint one.

Couples may also formulate exchange contracts, in which both partners work on changes they want to make in their relationship. For example, "If Jim fixes dinner twice a week, Sharon will mow the lawn." In working on reshuffling their housework responsibilities, they both make a change, and they tie the changes together with a contract.

> *Couples may formulate exchange contracts, in which both partners work on changes they want to make in their relationship*

K. Write an exchange contract that you would be willing to propose to your mate at the next group session.

_____

_____

In developing a contract with each other, it is important to watch for loopholes.

What happens when someone does not meet the contract? What happens if Jim fixed dinner and Sharon could not mow because it rained? If Jim did not fix the dinners, did that mean he had to do the mowing? Think ahead about what might happen and how you will handle it.

Does everyone have a role? It would not have been a good contract if Jim was expected to make a change with nothing in return from Sharon. That does not mean that spouses do not do things for each other if they do not get something in return, of course, but simply that it is only a contract if they both participate.

Is everyone committed to the contract? Contracts are gimmicky but effective ways to get change started in a relationship. They should always be freely entered by partners; neither should feel forced into a contract to appease the partner.

L. Analyze the extent you and your mate would honor the contract you wrote in exercise K by checking one of the sentences below.
❑ I would keep it, but my mate probably would not.
❑ My mate would keep it, but I probably would not.
❑ Neither of us would keep it.
❑ Both of us would keep it.

In summary, a contract can be written as follows:

	Wife	Husband
Desirable behaviors	mow	fix dinner
When/how often	1/wk.	2/wk.
Result	2 dinners by husband	wife will mow
When we will evaluate	May 10	May 10

COVENANTS AND CONTRACTS

Does calling a volunteer-grandparent program, giving each other points for sharing thoughts and perceptions, or exchanging cooking for mowing reflect a marriage covenant? In many ways, of course, it does not. A covenant is a promise, a commitment freely offered that can never be reduced to a contract. One phone call does not fulfill the promise to love each other actively and to let our love minister to others. Each descending level in the figure on the following page refines and makes more specific the one above it and, in so doing, loses some of the quality of the covenant promise.

A covenant is a promise, a commitment freely offered that can never be reduced to a contract

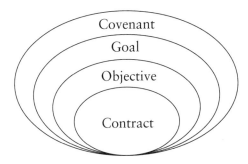

Yet in another sense, these simple contracts capture the essence of a covenant. They are actions and intentions. As covenant partners, we are taking responsibility for our lives together rather than letting them drift with happenstance. Contracts respect the freedom of each of us since we develop them together to reflect our shared plans to work actively toward change. They represent nurture of the relationship by the partners. They are hope.

M. Goals, objectives, and contracts are meant to encourage a couple toward purposeful change and growth. What qualities do you possess that contribute to a healthy marital growth climate?

_____

What qualities does your partner contribute to such a climate?

_____

N. How do you feel about the chances of your marriage's becoming a true partnership of love? Check your choice.
- ❑ Very optimistic
- ❑ Optimistic
- ❑ Mildly optimistic
- ❑ Mildly pessimistic
- ❑ Pessimistic
- ❑ Very pessimistic

SUMMARY

Covenant partners do not allow events or crises to determine their responses to each other. They choose to respond to what happens to them in such a way that their marriage is strengthened. Nine factors were given that influence a positive response to crisis by both partners.

An opportunity was given to review the major concepts and skills presented thus far in *Covenant Marriage: Partnership and Commitment*. As a result of looking again at all facets of a covenant relationship, you may have chosen to revise a portion of the original covenant developed in group session 1.

The relationship between covenants, goals, objectives, and contracts was explained, with an emphasis on how each contributes to the nurture of the relationship. They represent actions and intentions that help us take responsibility for our lives together.

As covenant partners, we are taking responsibility for our lives together rather than letting them drift with happenstance

CHECKPOINT

The following review exercise is designed to reveal whether you have achieved the learning goals for lesson 10. Answer each question. Correct answers are given after the final question.

1. The effect of a family crisis on a couple's relationship mainly results from—
   - ☐ a. the nature of the crisis;
   - ☐ b. the intensity of the crisis;
   - ☐ c. how couples choose to respond;
   - ☐ d. how others respond to the couple.

2. Factors that help a family come through a crisis stronger than before include all but which of the following?
   - ☐ a. Partners communicate clearly and directly.
   - ☐ b. A couple accepts that they are in a stressful situation.
   - ☐ c. Partners talk about the problem over and over.
   - ☐ d. A couple looks for who is to blame.

3. Answer *T* for *true* and *F* for *false*.
   - ___ a. During a crisis couples should pitch in wherever needed, regardless of whose job is whose.
   - ___ b. Couples in crisis should be in the situation together, not leave it up to one or the other to solve.
   - ___ c. Couples in crisis can often avoid the problem or crisis by avoiding each other.
   - ___ d. Partners should locate and use as many resources as possible to resolve the crisis.
   - ___ e. During a crisis partners should be allowed to ventilate their feelings or withdraw from each other.

4. Match the following.
   - ___ a. covenant   w. What kinds of changes we intend to make
   - ___ b. goal   x. Our best efforts to put our plans into action
   - ___ c. objective   y. Spells out what the outcome will be
   - ___ d. contract   z. A commitment freely offered

Now check your answers.
1. c
2. d
3. a. *T*, b. *T*, c. *F*, d. *T*, e. *F*
4. a. z, b. w, c. x, d. y

LOOKING AHEAD

Often a television show ends with the words "To be continued." This course is designed without an end! The final two lessons will affirm marriage enrichment as a lifelong process. Lesson 11 will help you discover resources for continuing to grow as covenant partners.

---

¹Hamilton I. McCubbin and Charles R. Figley, "Bridging Normative and Catastrophic Family Stress," in H. I. McCubbin and C. R. Figley, eds., *Coping with Normative Transitions*, vol. 1 of *Stress and the Family* (New York: Brunner/Mazel, 1983), 227.

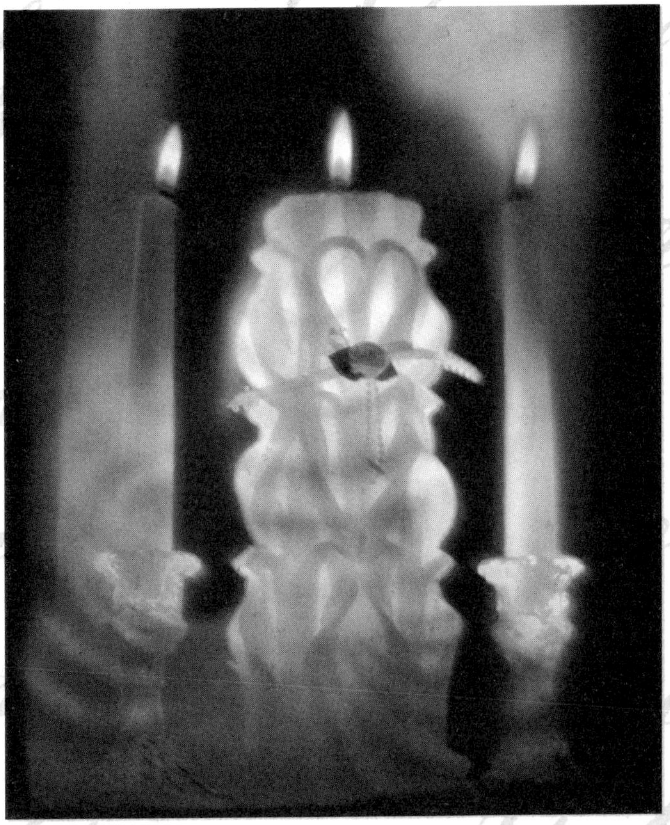

Unit 6

Couples Sharing and Supporting

PARTNERS ON PILGRIMAGE

Lesson 11

LOOKING BACK

The old adage "If at first you don't succeed, try, try again" applies to covenant marriage. Many of the concepts and skills we have learned in this course are new to us. They require different ways of relating to our partner and others. Practice and commitment are required to make them a part of our everyday lifestyles.

As we incorporate these new ways of *acting* into daily life, we will experience new ways of *feeling*. Covenant marriage focuses on the *will* to act responsibly, not how we feel at a given moment. Partners choose to respond to what happens to them in such a way that their marriage is strengthened. Nine factors were given in lesson 10 that influence a positive response to crisis by both partners.

A good way to begin implementing the characteristics of active love is to set goals, with accompanying objectives, that help chart a positive course for our marriage. Another way to choose responsible actions is to make a contract between partners that will encourage and reward appropriate behavior.

Remember, a covenant marriage does not just happen. A covenant marriage must be intentionally directed toward the ideal of a true partnership of love.

OVERVIEW

Do you remember your first experience behind the wheel of the family car alone, without the driving instructor or a parent to give support and advice? It's an exciting but scary feeling to be on your own.

Soon this marriage-enrichment course will end. You will have the opportunity in lesson 11 to plan how you and your partner will continue to enrich your marriage "on your own." You will find that many resources and people are available to help you have a pleasant and productive journey together. You are partners on pilgrimage!

When you complete this lesson, you will be able to—

- affirm enrichment as an ongoing process in the marriage relationship;
- identify resources for supporting marriage enrichment;
- describe the purpose and benefits of each resource;
- participate as a couple in a marriage-enrichment activity before the next group session;
- make a commitment to begin at least one of the activities identified and participate in it for one month as a trial.

Many resources and people are available to help you have a pleasant and productive journey together

GOALS OF MARRIAGE ENRICHMENT

As we stated in the introduction, the purposes of marriage enrichment include learning principles, ideas, and skills that can enhance marital relationships; assessing aspects of our marriage; celebrating the strengths of our marriage; and developing plans and working for change and growth in our relationship with our partner.

As helpful as a marriage-enrichment program may be, if couples relied on such a program alone to help them achieve the goals listed above, there would be a lot of stunted marriages. Enriching your marriage did not begin with this marriage-enrichment group, nor will it end when this group is over. Everyday experiences also offer opportunities for marriage enrichment.

Learning principles, ideas, and skills as we observe friends' marriages and the marriages of relatives. Sometimes the learning is negative: "Let's promise each other that we will never cut each other down or make jokes about each other in front of other people the way they do." Such negative learning can be a powerful push to change, particularly when we recognize with some horror that we do some of the same things we have observed others doing: "All they do is work at their jobs and spend money on gadgets and new sports equipment, like two kids blowing their whole allowance on toys. It all seems so self-centered, and I'm scared that we really aren't much different."

Learning can be positive, as well. During the first years of our marriage, we lived in a tiny apartment in student housing, where we quickly made friends with the couples around us. We greatly admired the "older couple" next door (they had been married for five years) because they had a loving, committed relationship. One evening we heard them arguing with raised voices. With dismay and fear for their marriage, we listened to them argue for more than 30 minutes. After this seemingly endless battle we heard them laughing. Ten minutes later they came to our door hand in hand and asked if we wanted to go get ice cream with them. We were absolutely amazed to learn that an argument did not have to destroy a relationship; in fact, they seemed even closer. That was the beginning of our learning that conflict can strengthen a relationship if handled properly.

These enriching experiences in everyday life are seldom planned: "Now we are going to listen to our neighbors argue and learn something about conflict." They simply require an openness to the opportunities for new experiences and new ideas all around us. They require us to consider our relationship as perpetually "under construction."

Everyday experiences offer opportunities for marriage enrichment

A. **What married couple served as a role model in the early years of your marriage?**

_____

Among your friends now, whose marriage do you most admire?

_____

Name one way you would like your marriage to be like theirs.

_____

Assessing aspects of our marriage. Anytime we experience something new, we know it is new because we compare it with previous experiences. For example, when we heard our friends arguing, we perked up our ears because our first response was "We never argue like that. We may get mad, but we don't really talk about it. Yet their marriage seems so happy. I wonder if we could be more like that instead of sulking at each other for hours when we are angry."

Assessment is also a key step in resolving conflict or facing troubles. "What is wrong here? What does each of us think and feel about this? How does our relationship need to change so that we can cope better with our differences?"

B. Who is more likely to bring up a need or a problem in your marriage? ❏ Me ❏ My mate

If my partner is the most likely one, do you value the assessing role as helpful to your marriage? ❏ Yes ❏ No

How can you demonstrate your gratitude for a partner who is willing to assess needed changes?

Celebrating our strengths. This goal is less likely to occur spontaneously in marriage. Think for a moment about your feet. How do they feel? Are they warm? Cool? If you are wearing socks or stockings, how does the material feel next to your skin? If you are wearing sandals, does the air feel gentle to your skin? Wiggle your toes. Are they all working right, or do any of them hurt? How strong are the muscles in your toes? These are strange questions; you were probably not even aware of your feet before your attention was drawn to them by these questions. You probably have not spent time recently thinking about how good your feet feel. The last time you thought about your feet was most likely the last time they hurt. Perhaps they hurt because you had been standing for a long while, or you had been walking or running. Or perhaps they were cold or wet, or you had a cramp in one of your toes.

Marriages are like feet; we think about them a lot when they hurt us but pretty much ignore them and let them carry us wherever we are going without giving them much thought when they feel all right. The saying "If it's not broken, don't fix it" goes one step farther when we are talking about feet and marriages to "If it's not broken and hurting, don't think about it."

Marriages, however, are not feet. Covenant relationships are celebrative relationships; we need to rejoice over what is good in our relationship in order to keep the problems and conflict in perspective and to give us the strength and hope to face whatever comes our way.

There are already some ritual celebrations of marriage, particularly the annual wedding anniversary. These need to be times not just to see a movie and eat out but times of true celebration of our relationship with each other. Looking back through wedding pictures and memory boxes from years past, recalling experiences, and telling each other, "I love you because . . ." help us celebrate our marriage.

Besides the annual celebration, we can also learn to stop and notice our re-

We need to rejoice over what is good in our relationship in order to keep the problems and conflict in perspective and to give us the strength and hope to face whatever comes our way

lationship just as you stopped a moment ago to notice your feet. It does not have to be an elaborate ritual but a simple sentence of appreciation or a compliment.

- "It makes me feel good that you bother to look as nice on Saturday when you are only going to be with me as you do the other days of the week when you are going to work."
- "I'm glad we talked about that last night, I feel a lot better today."
- "You are always so good to phone my mom and involve her in our family. I'm grateful that our families are families for both of us."

C. **Write a sentence of appreciation or a compliment you would like to give your mate.**

_____

_____

Developing plans and working for change and growth. This is also part of our daily lives. Yet often the plans we work on or the changes we concern ourselves with develop in the heat of a problem or a painful experience: "From now on, let's never cut each other down or make fun of each other in front of other people." This kind of plan may take root and grow and change the relationship in the desired direction. Many times, however, it gets lost in the shuffle of daily living. Contracts, even simple ones, can help us make these pledges a beginning of real change:

We agree to wait to express anger toward each other for times when we are not in public and then express it by describing what we are angry about instead of calling each other names. We will write a note on the calendar for three weeks from now to discuss over dinner how we are doing on our agreement.

D. **Look back at the contract you agreed to in group session 10. What progress has already been made—**

by you? _____

by your mate? _____

Plans also have to do with our use of resources—when to make major purchases, when to go on a trip, how much money we will save and how. They come as a part of sharing the same living space, money, and time.

Developing plans and working for change can enrich our relationships in other ways than dealing with problems or helping us share our resources in ways that most effectively meet our needs. We need to think and plan together about what we want our relationship to stand for beyond just avoiding problems and successfully navigating the waters of limited resources. It seems much easier to talk about what we want not to happen (embarrassing one another in front of friends, conflict that hurts us, an unplanned pregnancy) than it is to make the time and commitment ourselves to talk about something we

We need to think and plan together about what we want our relationship to stand for beyond just avoiding problems and successfully navigating the waters of limited resources

want to happen and how to plan for it (a relationship in which each of us feels appreciated and loved, a commitment to a shared goal).

E. Look back at the goals for your marriage you agreed to as a part of the previous group session. What have you already done this past week to begin implementing one of those goals?

_____

No marriage-enrichment program or reading resource or television documentary on marriage can replace couples' actively planning for ways the goals of marriage enrichment will be pursued in their relationship. Yet there are resources that can help us keep the commitment we have made to each other and that can provide aids as we press toward our goals.

RESOURCES FOR CONTINUING ENRICHMENT

Other Couples
Perhaps one of the most powerful resources for continuing enrichment available to you at the moment can be found in the new or deepened friendships you have developed with other couples in your marriage-enrichment group. You have shared your private thoughts, feelings, and experiences with one another. You have learned from others that you are not alone in your struggles, as well as helpful ideas and strategies that have helped others facing the same issues and situations. Learning that other marriages may be more like yours than the fictional, romantic marriages on television encourages you and gives you hope that any problems you have do not have to be terminal.

F. How did you feel at first about sharing your private thoughts, feelings, and experiences with others in the marriage-enrichment group? Check all of the words that apply.
❑ uncomfortable   ❑ exposed
❑ silly   ❑ tentative
❑ anxious   ❑ challenged
❑ excited   ❑ eager

How do you feel now about such sharing? Check all of the words that apply.
❑ more comfortable   ❑ grateful
❑ strengthened   ❑ helped
❑ relieved
❑ other: _____

In our society it is not acceptable to talk about the intimacies and troubles of our marriage in front of friends and family. Nothing can make others more uncomfortable than for a couple to argue in front of them or to talk openly about their problems or even their happiness with each other. Probably the unacceptability of airing our marital relationship in front of others started as a way to protect the marital relationship. Husbands and wives do not need to ventilate their frustration at each other over coffee with a friend or Mom in-

Learning that other marriages may be more like yours than the fictional, romantic marriages on television encourages you and gives you hope that any problems you have do not have to be terminal

stead of talking with each other and working it out. Partners need to trust each other to keep their confidences. Even court systems recognize this, not requiring partners to testify against each other.

In many respects, however, we have taken the privacy of marriage too far. We need to keep each other's trust and resolve problems with each other instead of spilling our feelings to others outside the relationship. But that does not mean we should never give others a glimpse of what our marriage is like. Sometimes the empathy of friends and family as we struggle with a difficult issue can be valuable. Or they may provide a different perspective or new ideas that are helpful.

G. Bert and Jean are visiting a couple from their Sunday School class. Suddenly the wife becomes angry over a remark her husband makes. Tension is in the air. What can/should Bert and Jean do in such a situation? Check one.
❑ Ignore it and change the subject.
❑ "Who am I to help? I've got problems of my own."
❑ Pitch in and help them resolve the conflict.
❑ Be available but not pushy if they need to talk it out.
❑ Talk with them later individually.
❑ Other: _____

We aim not just to get help or ideas from others but also to give our own support and encouragement to others in return

When can sharing our marriage with others be helpful instead of harmful? Sharing that simply ventilates our frustration about our partner tears down our marital relationship; it does nothing to repair the damage done by the anger and destructive conflict between us. Sharing with others outside our relationship that aims at getting resources to help us deal with that which troubles us or to celebrate the blessings of our relationship can be helpful. Such sharing can happen between couples who have participated in a marriage-enrichment group with one another. They know one another's strengths and weaknesses and can encourage and challenge one another to continue growing and developing their gifts as covenant partners through the grace of a covenant-making God. Such sharing is not one-sided. We aim not just to get help or ideas from others but also to give our own support and encouragement to others in return.

H. How would you feel if you knew that your partner was discussing your marriage with a good friend? Check one.
❑ Betrayed
❑ Grateful for the help
❑ Embarrassed
❑ Wouldn't bother me
❑ Think it's a good idea

What benefits might come from sharing marital concerns with a trusted friend?

_____

If a continuing supportive relationship with other couples in your group interests you, you may want to discuss it in this week's group session. Several couples may want to meet together once each month to share a potluck supper. Each couple could take time to share progress on objectives and goals, receive the group's suggestions and encouragement, and make plans for the following month. An appointed leader would be an asset, or perhaps leadership might be rotated among members. This will ensure that the group stays on the path you plan together.

There may be other meeting times or forms that would better suit your needs and the needs of the group. Even if meeting together on a regular basis is not feasible, plan ways to check with one another, to encourage one another in the weeks and months ahead.

This will be a difficult time for many couples; you have poured a great deal of energy into your marriage these past few weeks as you have read and interacted with these materials and participated in enrichment activities both in and outside the group sessions. Other demands have been put on hold. As you return to life as usual, the dreams and possibilities of these weeks of marriage enrichment may fade and seem unrealistic or impossible. Communication with your partner will have a tendency to revert to old patterns. The marriage relationship may again get just the leftovers of time and energy.

Even if meeting together on a regular basis is not feasible, plan ways to check with one another, to encourage one another in the weeks and months ahead

I. Whoa! If you are determined to keep this from happening ...

Name one old habit you resolve not to revert to.

_____

Name one new skill you intend to develop into a good habit.

_____

Encouragement and sharing with other couples can make the difference between this marriage-enrichment experience being the beginning of life change or simply a workshop that seemed good at the time but did not really make a difference.

If meeting regularly as a group seems impossible, here are other ways you can continue to encourage one another.

- Form buddy groups of two or three couples each who can share dinner together in an inexpensive restaurant or meet together for dessert once a month or as planned. It helps to commit yourself to a date and time beforehand instead of leaving it on a "Call us when you want to get together" basis.
- Plan a reunion in three months, a potluck supper in someone's home, or simply a meeting. Appoint someone in the group to lead.
- Make an effort to care for one another. Call a couple in the group who have small children and offer to care for the children one evening while they have time alone. Send an article, a cartoon, or a movie or book suggestion to a couple you think will find it useful.

J. Which of the ideas presented above seems most practical? Most helpful?

_____

Which will you probably do?

_____

Finally, there are many resources available through churches that you and your mate or your group may want to investigate.

Couples Bible Study
HomeLife, a monthly family magazine, provides daily devotional passages and family devotional activities. The magazine *Open Windows* can also be used in Bible study together. Bible study as a couple can encourage you in the spiritual discipline of marriage and can offer a structured time of reflecting on the good gift of marriage.*

K. Secure a copy of *HomeLife*. Review the family devotionals for the month.

Couples Prayer Retreat
A prayer retreat enables partners to grow spiritually by beginning or deepening a prayer partnership. Together you can discover how prayer can help you grow individually and as a couple. Such a retreat can be held in a retreat setting, beginning one evening and ending the next day. Prayer retreats are usually group experiences.

You and your partner may want to plan a private prayer retreat together. In a quiet setting away from the demands of daily living, you can make time for reflection and quiet receptivity to the Lord's guidance in your lives together, and you can talk and pray together and individually about an important decision or plans for the future.

You and your partner may want to plan a private prayer retreat together

L. Evaluate your prayer life as a couple by circling the number that indicates your response to each statement below.

	Yes	Somewhat	No
1. My partner and I pray together on a regular basis.	1	2	3
2. We rely on prayer together to help us make decisions, both large and small.	1	2	3
3. We are able to express our deepest thoughts and longings in our prayer time.	1	2	3
4. Both of us equally desire a time to pray together.	1	2	3
5. After we pray together, we feel closer to each other and to God.	1	2	3

Marriage-Enrichment Retreat
A marriage-enrichment retreat provides an opportunity to enjoy being together and to celebrate marriage with other couples. The retreat model begins after

151

dinner on the first day and concludes at noon on the third day. The program focuses on communication, giving and receiving nurture, recreation, intimacy, and worship.

A variety of resources is available for use on a retreat. An excellent resource for this purpose is *The Five Love Languages* by Gary Chapman. This study teaches couples how to enrich their marriages by identifying and practicing their spouses' love languages.*

M. How would you feel about the prospect of having a marriage-enrichment retreat for your church? Jot down your thoughts about—

Benefits: _____

Possible topics: _____

Place: _____

When: _____

Who might come: _____

Reading and discussion are useful ways to keep on track in enriching a relationship

Group and Couples Studies

You may find that reading and discussion are useful ways to keep on track in enriching a relationship. One couple, for example, takes a book about marriage and family relationships or another topic particularly relevant to what they are focusing on in their marriage with them on trips. They then take turns reading aloud while the other drives. Traveling in the car offers plenty of time for discussion and reflection.

Not all enriching readings focus directly on marriage relationships. Parents will find reading and talking together about child development and parenting to be meaningful and helpful in their marriage. Materials related to your task together as well as the intimacy between you will be valuable.

N. Carla loves to read, but Howard is an outdoorsman. Carla has decided to read something about marriage and family life every week. Should Carla attempt to share what she is reading with Howard? ❑ Yes ❑ No

How should Howard react to Carla's attempts to share what she has learned?

_____

_____

How might such sharing be most effectively carried out in your marriage?

_____

_____

In addition to reading together as a couple, consider taking additional marriage-enrichment courses similar to *Covenant Marriage: Partnership and Commitment*. Possibilities include the following.

- *Communication and Intimacy: Covenant Marriage* by Gary Chapman and Betty Hassler. This 13-session course equips couples to strengthen their relationships by developing communication skills and achieving greater intimacy.*
- *Building Relationships: A Discipleship Guide for Married Couples* by Gary Chapman. This 12-session course teaches couples sharing and communication skills and guides them to a deeper relationship with God.*
- *The Five Love Languages* by Gary Chapman. This 2-session study teaches couples to enrich their marriages by learning and practicing their spouses' love languages.*
- *Making Love Last Forever* by Gary Smalley. This 12-session study teaches couples how to make their love grow throughout their married lives.*
- *I Take Thee to Be My Spouse: Bible Study for Newlyweds*, compiled by David Apple. This study provides 26 weeks of Bible study focusing on the needs and interests of newlyweds.*

O. A group study I would like to participate in is—

Many churches and denominations provide conferences and retreats for married couples

National Conferences

Many churches and denominations provide conferences and retreats for married couples. The church staff or the denomination's family-ministry leader can help you find out when such events take place.

Fall Festival of Marriage is a national conference conducted on weekends in the fall at a number of locations. These events feature conferences, music, worship, and Bible study in a relaxing retreat setting. Another national marriage-enrichment event is the Toward a Growing Marriage seminar, which features Gary Chapman. This seminar teaches couples biblical principles they need to grow in their relationships. You may obtain information about these two national marriage-enrichment events by writing to Marriage-Enrichment Events, MSN 151; LifeWay Christian Resources; 127 Ninth Avenue, North; Nashville, TN 37234-0151; by faxing (615) 251-5058; or by emailing bgoad@lifeway.com.

THE CHOICES ARE YOURS

Many opportunities for marriage enrichment are available. You can use resources prepared by others, and you can find ways to think creatively about the experiences you share each day. You can participate in a retreat, or the two of you can spend Saturday with a picnic lunch and bicycles and a commitment to pray and talk together about God's blessings and calling in your life.

The key to selecting among the many opportunities is your own needs. If your lives are pressured by outside demands, the structure and ritual of a calendared time, 7:00–10:00 on Tuesday evening or the first Saturday of every month, and of a structured resource, such as the devotional ideas in *HomeLife* and *Open Windows*, may be invaluable. As attention to your marriage begins to pay off with more intimacy and more effectiveness in your life together, the focus on enrichment will come more easily.

SUMMARY

Marriage enrichment is a continuous process in a covenant-marriage relationship. The goals of marriage enrichment include learning principles, ideas, and skills that can enhance marital relationships, assessing aspects of our marriage, celebrating the strengths of our marriage, and developing plans and working for change and growth in our relationship with our partner.

The resources for continuing marriage enrichment are numerous. They include friendships with other couples in your marriage-enrichment group and a variety of resources available through churches. Family devotionals are regular features of *HomeLife* magazine. Churches may want to offer couples prayer retreats or marriage-enrichment retreats. National conferences, like Fall Festivals of Marriage, are offered annually. Couples may choose to participate with other couples in book studies or group marriage-enrichment courses. Or they may read and discuss as a couple books related to marriage and family living.

Couples should select at least one method whereby they can affirm and strengthen their commitment to each other on a regular basis.

CHECKPOINT

The following review exercise is designed to reveal whether you have achieved the learning goals for lesson 11. Answer each question. Correct answers are given after the final question.

1. Marriage enrichment is a process that should occur—
   - ❑ a. at least once in a given marital relationship;
   - ❑ b. every three to five years;
   - ❑ c. annually;
   - ❑ d. continuously.
2. The goals of marriage enrichment include all but which of the following?
   - ❑ a. Learning principles, ideas, and skills that can enhance marital relationships
   - ❑ b. Assessing aspects of your marriage
   - ❑ c. Celebrating the strengths of your marriage
   - ❑ d. Working for change and growth in your partner
3. Match the following marriage-enrichment resources with its definition.
   - ___ a. Couples Bible study
   - ___ b. *Communication and Intimacy: Covenant Marriage*
   - ___ c. Fall Festival of Marriage
   - (1) A group marriage-enrichment course
   - (2) A national marriage-enrichment event
   - (3) A marriage-enrichment exercise for couples centered on the study of Scripture

4. Which of the marriage-enrichment activities listed in lesson 11 could you participate in during the coming week?

_____

Now check your answers.
1. d
2. d

> *Marriage enrichment is a continuous process in a covenant-marriage relationship*

3. a (3), b. (1), c. (2)
4. **Personal response**

LOOKING AHEAD

Do you recall this observation about a married couple from page 145 of this lesson? "All they do is work at their jobs and spend money on gadgets and new sports equipment, like two kids blowing their whole allowance on toys. It all seems so self-centered, and I'm scared that we really aren't much different."

How can we keep our marriages from being self-serving? How can marriage be a means to minister to others? In lesson 12 we will examine attitudes and actions that will enable us to bless others through our marriages.

---

*Order resources by writing to Customer Service Center; MSN 113; 127 Ninth Avenue, North; Nashville, TN 37234-0113; by emailing customerservice@lifeway.com; by faxing (615) 251-5933; by ordering online at www.lifeway.com; or by calling toll free (800) 458-2772.

MINISTERING THROUGH MARRIAGE

Lesson 12

> *The world needs the witness of a couple dedicated to each other and to God*

LOOKING BACK

Marriage enrichment is a continuous process in a covenant marriage. A variety of resources is available for continuing marriage enrichment. Do you recall the resources you learned about in lesson 11?

You may be looking forward to a couples prayer retreat or a marriage-enrichment retreat. Perhaps you know of a church that is planning a family-life conference.

What specific marriage-enrichment activity did you and your partner participate in during the past few days? What are you committed to doing for one month as a trial? Keep in mind that marriage enrichment does not usually happen by accident; it must be planned.

OVERVIEW

This course began with the characteristics of God's covenant with the nation Israel. We were reminded that the covenant relationship God established with His people was meant to bless all peoples of the earth. God's covenant was not to be hoarded for the pleasure and fulfillment of Israel alone.

In a similar way, our covenant marriages are not to be hoarded for the enjoyment of ourselves and our families alone. All of our God-given resources are meant to be shared with a needy world. Surely the world needs the witness of a couple dedicated to each other and to God.

As you read this final lesson, think of ways your marriage relationship can bless others.

When you complete this lesson, you will be able to—
- define *marriage* as a vehicle of ministry;
- list ways couples can minister through their marriages;
- assess the appropriateness of each form of ministry for your marriage relationship;
- make a commitment to select and initiate at least one ministry, agreeing to try it for two months.

A CREATURE OF HABIT

A city zoo was able to expand because of gifts from a generous donor. Part of the expansion was to add a polar bear. The polar bear was not due to arrive until January l. By then the new polar-bear area, with rocks and swimming pool and caves, would be completed. But the polar bear unexpectedly arrived three months early, in late October. With no other choice, the polar bear had to remain in a somewhat enlarged cage that was placed in the polar-bear area while the construction crew hastily worked to complete his new home. Hour after hour the polar bear paced in his cage; he walked six loping steps the length of the cage, reared and turned around on his hind legs, walked the same six loping steps back, reared and turned and walked six more paces—over and over. Day after day, week after week as the construction crew worked, the bear paced.

People came to watch the men working and the bear pacing. It seemed as though the bear did not even see the bars of his cage anymore; he paced his six paces and reared and paced again as though the pacing had been a part of who he was from the very beginning.

One little boy had come to watch the bear day after day. At first he felt sad for the bear in the cage in the warmth of late fall. Then one day he wondered aloud: "I wonder if that bear will always be like that. I wonder if he will always go six steps and turn around and go six steps back, over and over. Maybe he won't know how to do anything else anymore. Maybe he won't know what to do outside a cage. Maybe he'll just stay in that same spot, walking six steps back and forth, back and forth."

The long-awaited day finally came. The bear's new home was completed. The cage was made in such a way that a crane sitting outside the fence could lift the top of the cage straight up. The bars were firmly attached to the cage's roof, so that only the floor would be left and the bear would be free to walk off in any direction he pleased. The little boy and many others came to watch with excitement. What would the bear do when the bars were lifted? Would he run for a dive in the water of his new pool? Would he climb to the top of the rocks? Or would he stay on the floor of the cage, take six steps, rear and turn to go back, over and over? As the observers held their breath, the bars were slowly raised until the bars of the bear's cage were gone. And the bear ...

Possibilities come our way for breaking the bonds of habit

A. How would you like for this story to end? Take a few moments before reading on to think about the bear. Write the ending you think belongs to this story.

Bears are not the only ones who pace cages. Our patterns of living, our ways of relating to each other, our habits, even our goals and dreams may often be six steps, a turn, and a repeat. Moments of decision come, however, when the bars are lifted. Possibilities come our way for breaking the bonds of habit. The limitations on our thinking and dreaming are cracked open, and we glimpse an expanse of ideas and dreams and ways of living.

B. If you were the bear, which option would you most likely choose? Check one.
  ❏ **Take six steps back and forth as usual.**
  ❏ **Venture slowly into new surroundings.**
  ❏ **Immediately enjoy the vistas of opportunity.**

Changing our ways can be frightening, though. There is security in tried-and-true ways. We are safe in our six-pace patterns, and sometimes being safe may be more important than exploring possibilities.

Perhaps your experiences in your *Covenant Marriage* group have made you feel like that bear must have felt. Possibilities for new boundaries to your marriage relationship lie before you. The bars of habit, of role definitions have been yanked up or at least been given a good shaking. They are loose. What will you do now?

The analogy cannot be pushed too far. The choices we make are not as clear-cut as the choice between the narrow box of a cage and the freedom to roam and swim and frolic in the sunshine. Some of our patterns, our roles, our habits we like and want to keep. We have been intentional in structuring our lives the way they are.

C. What is a pattern of relating that you like and intend to keep?

_____

Will your choices make your mate feel—
❑ **unhappy?**
❑ **pleased?**

There are also times to change and times not to change. If you and your partner are experiencing upheaval and stress from other quarters of your life, it may be a time to embrace the steady, reliable patterns of living in your marriage and leave change for another time. Just remember that the bars are loose when you want to give them a shaking.

D. If this is not an appropriate time for major changes in your lifestyle, explain why.

_____

_____

When might be a good time in the future?

_____

Imagine for a moment, then, that your marriage is that pacing bear. What are the bars on your marriage's cage? Limited styles of relating to each other? Goals and dreams that have not changed since you married? What do you glimpse beyond the "bars," perhaps as a result of this *Covenant Marriage* course? How would you like to write the end of the story for yourself?

E. Write one "bar" on your marriage's "cage" that keeps you from functioning in your marriage the way you want to.

_____

158

What do you glimpse beyond that "bar" that makes you wish it were gone?

_____

_____

What could you do to remove the "bar"?

_____

_____

MINISTERING MARRIAGES

Lesson 11 focused on the continuing process of enrichment after this group ends. Enrichment can come from more than just turning our attention inward toward our relationship with each other as spouses. We can also continue to enrich our relationship by turning outward as partners in ministry, in the tasks and purposes to which we are called by God. Marriages are measured by their fruit, not just by how intimate, fulfilling, and healthy their foliage looks (see Matthew 3:10; 21:18-19; Luke 13:6-9).

Lesson 5 focused on the fruit of marriage as tasks and purposes that give meaning to your life together. In that lesson you identified the tasks and purposes that are important in your marriage. Perhaps you also made plans for developing or continuing what you have already begun together. But you have talked together and shared in the group a great deal since that session. You may remember what you wrote in that session, but before you review it, take some time to work through the following statements. Later you can compare how you and your partner think and feel about your relationship now and how you did then.

Identify the importance of your relationship now. No one else can tell you what the purpose and focus of your marriage are to be. Others can share their perspectives with you and tell you how they see your gifts and strengths; but you and your partner, as you pray for guidance and listen receptively for God's word in your lives, decide what your marriage will stand for. How is God calling you and your partner to minister in the lives of others and in the world around you?

Look for threads of meaning in your common life. God often speaks to us in a quiet voice through the common events of our lives. We can look back through our lives together and see the work of the Holy Spirit even when we were not aware of it at the time. What have you and your partner done together that has brought special meaning to your lives? How do you see God working in your shared life? What is important to you? What do you want your marriage to stand for?

F. Think back over the past week. What decisions have you made together? What activities have you engaged in together? What plans have you made that give your relationship meaning and purpose? Describe one example.

_____

_____

How is God calling you and your partner to minister in the lives of others and in the world around you?

Look for the fruit of your joint effort. Imagine what the world would be like if you and your partner had not married. What difference has your marriage made in the lives of others and in the world around you? How has your marriage affected the lives of friends and family? Church? Community?

Expect purposes to change with time. Every day we make decisions that alter the course we walk together. The change in direction today may seem only slight, but it may have tremendous impact in the years ahead. As you begin a journey on foot, you may alter your path only one degree to the south, which means only inches of difference in the beginning but miles of difference in the end. Every decision we make together affects our ministry, our task, our relationship with the world around us in some way.

Our purposes also change with changes in the world around us. Neighbors come and go, jobs change, and others need us in different ways.

G. Review your responses to exercises M, O, and P in lesson 5 several weeks ago (pp. 75–76). How would your responses today be different or similar?

_____

_____

_____

Your group will want to support or encourage one another or even join forces with one another in the tasks and purposes you have embraced as couples. The following summaries of resources for groups may fit what you and your group would like to plan together, or they may suggest to you other ideas for how you can support and encourage one another and perhaps even work together as a network of couples in ministry.

Couples Support Group
In the previous group session you may have made plans to continue meeting together in a less formal way to support and encourage one another in the processes of marriage enrichment. As a part of that continuing ministry with one another, you may want to covenant together as a group to tell one another about the work each couple is doing. You can offer to one another needed support, encouragement, suggestions, and even challenge. There may be ways you can join your efforts as individual couples and share a commitment.

One group, for example, decided to commit themselves to developing a simpler lifestyle and to use their resources of time and money to meet the needs of others. They began by developing a system of sharing resources, with each couple listing items they currently had that they would be willing to share with others in the group, such as tools, freezer space, infrequently used appliances and kitchen equipment (ice-cream maker, pressure canner, etc.), and sports equipment. They also listed services they would be willing to trade, such as carpentry, child care, do-it-yourself plumbing, car repair, and so on. The money they saved from sharing was sent to a mission center to sponsor an after-school tutoring-and-activities program for inner-city children. In addition, several of the couples worked in the program, and the group developed friendships with some of the children's families.

Every decision we make together affects our ministry, our task, our relationship with the world around us in some way

H. Can you think of a type of group you and your mate might enjoy belonging to?

_____

Be prepared to share your ideas at the next group session.

Other Group Events
Your group might like to support or request that a church offer an event or program such as *Covenant Marriage* that relates directly to your tasks as a couple. Several examples are listed here.
Parenting by Grace. Parenting by Grace resembles *Covenant Marriage;* it is an enrichment program for parents. The course helps couples use the gift of God's grace as they love, affirm, discipline, and guide their children to mature, responsible Christian living.
Topical issues in parenting. Couples who have identified parenting as a primary task in their relationship may also have specific concerns they would like to address. Parents may want to explore, for example, how their family can become a force for peace and justice in their community and world. Parents of older children and adolescents may be concerned about the use of drugs and alcohol and how they can help their children face peer pressure. They may find it helpful to work together as a group in a concerted effort to help their children face these temptations responsibly.

Couples may have specific concerns they would like to address

I. Check any of the following issues you want to study with a group of couples in the future.

Husband-Wife Relationships
❑ How to better communicate with my spouse
❑ How to work out appropriate husband-wife roles
❑ How to handle conflict in a Christian manner
❑ How to achieve sexual happiness in marriage
❑ How to handle money/family finances
❑ How to manage a two-career marriage
❑ How to have a meaningful spiritual partnership

Family Relationships
❑ How to effectively discipline my children
❑ How to schedule more time for the family/manage time
❑ How to build good relationships with in-laws
❑ How to communicate Christian values to children
❑ How to talk with my children about sex
❑ How to develop an adult relationship with your parents or your children
❑ How to care for aging parents
❑ How to plan for parenting
❑ How to cope when one parent travels extensively
❑ How to manage change effectively
❑ How to build a positive self-image in children

Couples night out. Couples night out provides opportunities for marriage enrichment through witnessing to and reaching for Bible study marriage partners who are not already involved. Other couples are invited to be involved in an evening of fellowship and fun, couple time, and a brief devotional Bible study. Couples night out enables couples to reach out to other couples in which one or both partners are not active in Sunday School or other church programs.

J. Name two or three couples who are not involved in Bible study and who might respond to an invitation to meet with you for a couples night out.

_____

Hospitality group. Your group may share a commitment to develop the gift of hospitality. There may be a specific group in need for whom you want to pray and open your homes and your hearts and whom you jointly want to sponsor. These may include refugee families, individuals or families in crisis who have come to the attention of a church or community ministry in your area, a child who needs foster care, elderly persons living alone or in a nursing facility, or mentally ill or retarded persons who have no family and need someone to provide friendship and support. A hospitality group is a kind of mission group. Many other mission-group opportunities could be developed.

Family cluster. Your group may be concerned about the isolation of single persons, elderly persons, and even families in your area. You may want to develop small "family" units, in which single persons and families can group together to covenant with one another to be a "family."

K. Name one or more persons in the following categories who need friendship and might respond to a hospitality group or family cluster.

Widow: _____

Widower: _____

Single adult: _____

Handicapped: _____

Mentally disadvantaged: _____

Economically disadvantaged: _____

Elderly couple: _____

New in town: _____

PLANNING AHEAD

In the weeks ahead you will probably see the bars of habit and commitments and responsibilities that have shaped your marriage up to this point descend again. All of the household tasks and patterns of living that have been put off while you participated in the *Covenant Marriage* group will face you. It will

> *There may be a specific group in need whom you jointly want to sponsor*

be easy to go back to a six-paces style in your relationship with each other. As exciting as some of the possibilities for a deeper commitment to ministry together seem at this point, there will probably not be enough time for them—unless you plan for them now.

The final group session will focus attention on any plans you want to make together in support of individual couples' ministries or in shared ministry as a group. You and your partner may also want to make plans about how you want to turn the dreams and goals you have discussed together into reality. Perhaps you would like to make a commitment together to develop some objectives that will move you toward the goal of a meaningful shared ministry as covenant partners.

L. Look at the goals and objectives you and your partner agreed to in group session 10. Which of these is a shared ministry?

_____

_____

If none of them represents a shared ministry, take time to work together to develop objectives that will point you toward your shared-ministry goals.

Keep in mind the following pointers in writing objectives.
• Be specific. Who will do what?
• Specify a time. Two months may be an appropriate amount of time for starting work on goals. Write on the family calendar when you will review your objectives.
• Involve both partners. You both may have significant individual ministry responsibilities, but these objectives need to speak to your shared ministry as covenant partners.
• Be realistic. Other demands and commitments you have, both as individuals and as a couple, are also important. Make sure that what you spell out to implement is do-able so that you don't become discouraged and give up. Start small and increase your expectations later.

M. Write a shared-ministry goal and its objectives.

Goal: _____

_____

_____

Objectives: _____

_____

_____

_____

> *As exciting as some of the possibilities for a deeper commitment to ministry together seem at this point, there will probably not be enough time for them—unless you plan for them now*

KEEPING MARRIAGE IN PERSPECTIVE

Armed with objectives and plans as a couple and as a group of couples, you are finishing the *Covenant Marriage* course. We have lifted your marriage relationship out of the context of church and family for a time of careful examination, assessment, celebration, and challenge. Now it is time to place marriage back in its context. This may have been a time of greater closeness and intimacy between you and your partner and perhaps a time of heightened conflict as you carefully looked at your differences and your needs.

When your focus turns from marriage to the other aspects of your life as individuals, you may feel let down as the level of intimacy you have felt with each other and even the conflict and intensity of your relationship return to the levels prior to the *Covenant Marriage* course. It is time to go back to the valleys of service. There are going to be dry spells, and you may feel even more distant from each other than you have before, since you have tasted new possibilities.

Yes, you have new skills you can use in the situations and experiences that lie before you. Although during much of the time in the weeks ahead your relationship may feel the way it did before, it is different because of what you have learned about each other, because of the choices you can now make about how to respond to the stresses and crises and opportunities in your life together. You are covenant partners, facing life and its challenges together.

> *Now it is time to place marriage back in its context*

N. How has your perspective on your relationship changed since the beginning of this marriage-enrichment course, if it has?

_____

_____

_____

What changes do you hope and pray for in the weeks and months to come?

_____

_____

_____

What slight changes (or big changes) do you need to make to begin moving in the way you feel God leading you as a couple?

_____

_____

_____

SUMMARY

Now that this marriage-enrichment course is coming to a close, possibilities for new horizons in your marriage relationship lie before you. Bars of habit, role definitions, and complacency, to name a few, have been loosed. What will you do now?

We can continue to enrich our marriage relationships by turning outward as partners in ministry, in the tasks and purposes to which we are called by God. Plans you may have made for shared ministry as a result of lesson 5 were re-examined and expanded. New goals and objectives may have been determined that will point you toward your shared-ministry tasks.

A number of ways you can minister through your marriage were explored, including a couples support group, other group events, couples night out, hospitality groups, and family clusters.

You were encouraged to plan ahead in order to turn the dreams and goals you have discussed together into reality. Choices that lie ahead can be responded to positively because you are covenant partners, facing life and its challenges together.

Choices that lie ahead can be responded to positively because you are covenant partners, facing life and its challenges together

CHECKPOINT

The following review exercise is designed to reveal whether you have achieved the learning goals for lesson 12. Answer each question. Correct answers are given after the final question.

1. Our marriage resembles a bear loosed from his cage as a result of this marriage-enrichment course because—
   ❑ a. possibilities for new opportunities lie before us;
   ❑ b. we are frightened by the new boundaries;
   ❑ c. we may decide to stay in the cage;
   ❑ d. we must slowly and carefully explore new territories.

2. Fill in the blanks in the following sentences that explain how a couple can discover avenues of shared ministry.
   a. Identify the _____ of your _____ now.
   b. Look for _____ of _____ in your _____ life.
   c. Look for the _____ of your _____ effort.
   d. Expect _____ to change with _____.

3. Define the following types of shared ministry.

   a. Couples support group: _____

   b. Couples night out: _____

   c. Hospitality group: _____

   d. Family cluster: _____

4. Name at least one ministry you and your mate want to try for two months.

165

Now check your answers.

1. a
2. a. importance, relationship; b. threads, meaning, common; c. fruit, joint; d. purposes, time
3. a. a shared commitment by several couples to support and encourage one another; b. an effort to reach couples not involved in Bible study through an evening of fun, fellowship, and Bible study; c. opening your home to individuals or groups who need friendship and support; d. small family units in your congregation that include persons who need a family relationship
4. Personal response

LOOKING AHEAD

Congratulations! You are to be commended for completing this course. Please plan to keep this guide on hand as a reference in the coming months. Make a commitment to take it out in one month and glance over the completed exercises. You will be encouraged as you note progress on goals and changes that indicate growth on the part of you and your partner.

THE COVENANT-MARRIAGE MOVEMENT

Covenant Marriage is more than a resource; it is a movement of God among couples across America and around the world. God has instilled in the hearts of couples from every walk of life the need to affirm His intent for marriage. Couples are aware of the need to take seriously the vows made on their wedding day. They want their love to last for a lifetime.

Churches are pulling together in their respective communities to offer a unified commitment to strengthen marriages and families by initiating community-marriage policies or community-marriage covenants.

In a day when "no-fault" divorces run rampant, several states have taken a stand to uplift the importance of the permanence of marriage. These states have passed laws that provide couples the option of entering a covenant marriage, which requires marriage preparation and, except for extreme cases, extensive counseling before a divorce can be finalized. Covenant Marriage has become a movement supported by government, religious, community, and educational leaders.

God is at work in the lives of couples, and we are excited that you and your spouse are among those couples. In signing this covenant, you and your spouse join thousands of other couples across the nation and around the world in affirming the importance of a covenant-marriage relationship. But more personally, you commit or recommit to each other to remain steadfast in the unconditional love God expects of you and provides for you.

If you are preparing for marriage, this statement can become your vow to God and to each other before God. You may want to consider including it in your wedding ceremony.

We suggest that you sign, date, cut out, and laminate the covenant to keep with you as a gentle reminder of your commitment to each other.

OUR COVENANT MARRIAGE

Believing that marriage is a covenant intended by God to be a lifelong relationship between a man and a woman, we vow to God, each other, our families, and our community to remain steadfast in unconditional love, reconciliation, and sexual purity, while purposefully growing in our covenant-marriage relationship.

_____   _____
Name   Date

_____   _____
Name   Date

167

970 AM 90-7 AM 970 AM
8:00
www.lote.org

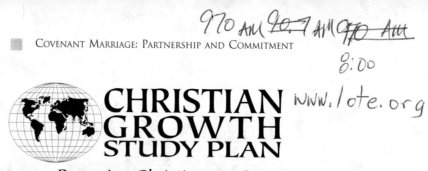

CHRISTIAN GROWTH STUDY PLAN

Preparing Christians to Serve

In the Christian Growth Study Plan (formerly the Church Study Course) *Covenant Marriage: Partnership and Commitment* is a resource for course credit in the subject area Home/Family in the Christian Growth category of diploma plans. To receive credit, read the book; complete the learning activities; attend group sessions; show your work to your pastor, a staff member, or a church leader; then complete the following information. This page may be duplicated. Send the completed page to:

Christian Growth Study Plan, MSN 117
127 Ninth Avenue, North
Nashville, TN 37234-0117
Fax (615) 251-5067

For information about the Christian Growth Study Plan, refer to the current *Christian Growth Study Plan Catalog*. Your church office may have a copy. If not, request a free copy from the Christian Growth Study Plan office, (615) 251-2525.

Covenant Marriage: Partnership and Commitment
COURSE NUMBER: CG-0199

PARTICIPANT INFORMATION

Social Security Number (USA ONLY) | Personal CGSP Number* | Date of Birth (MONTH, DAY, YEAR)

Name (First, Middle, Last)
☐ Mr. ☐ Miss
☐ Mrs. ☐

Home Phone

Address (Street, Route, or P.O. Box) | City, State, or Province | Zip/Postal Code

CHURCH INFORMATION

Church Name

Address (Street, Route, or P.O. Box) | City, State, or Province | Zip/Postal Code

CHANGE REQUEST ONLY

☐ Former Name

☐ Former Address | City, State, or Province | Zip/Postal Code

☐ Former Church | City, State, or Province | Zip/Postal Code

Signature of Pastor, Conference Leader, or Other Church Leader | Date

*New participants are requested but not required to give SS# and date of birth. Existing participants, please give CGSP# when using SS# for the first time. Thereafter, only one ID# is required. **Mail to:** Christian Growth Study Plan, 127 Ninth Ave., North, Nashville, TN 37234-0117. Fax: (615)251-5067